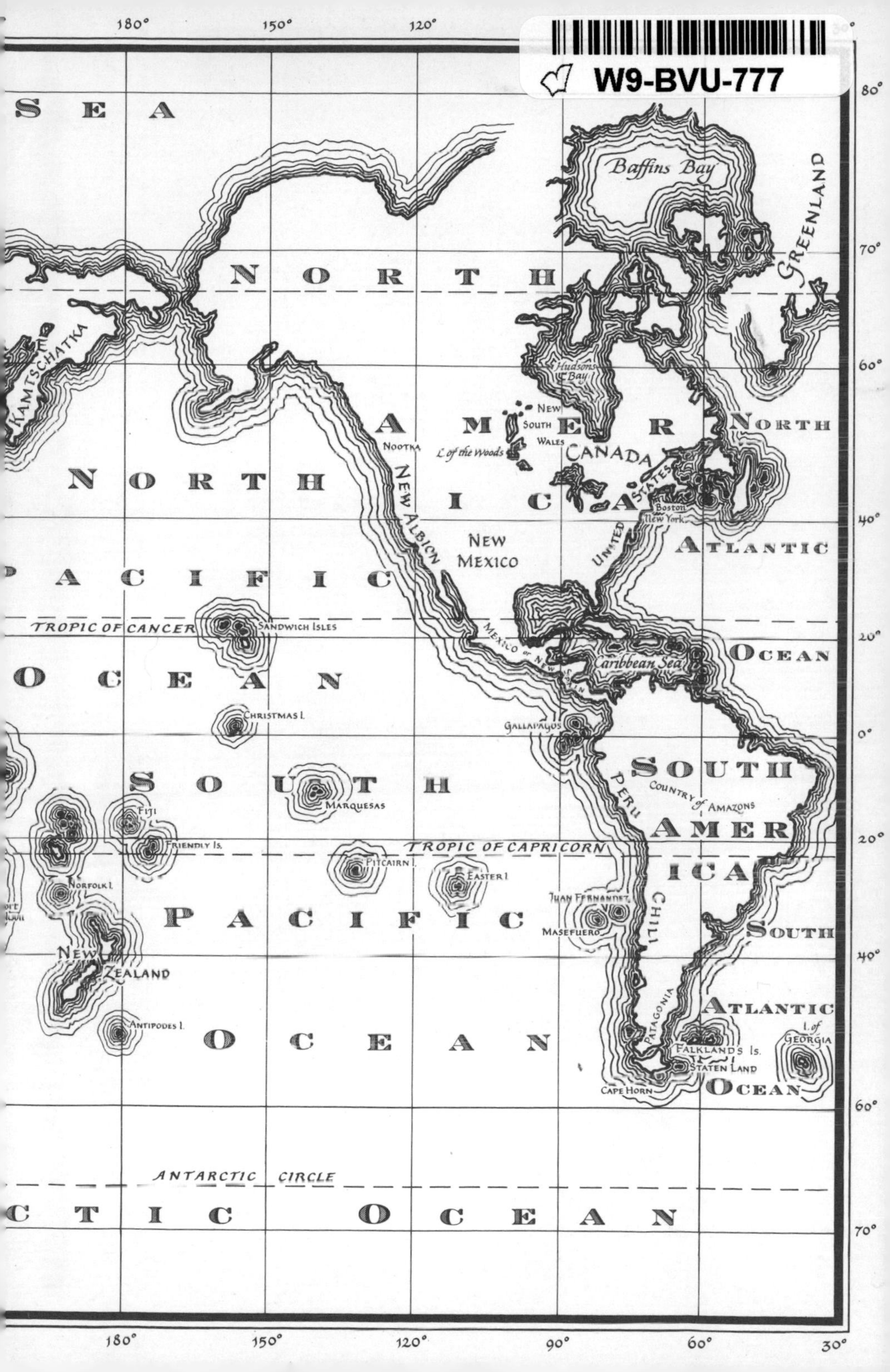

W9-BVU-777
180°
150°
120°
30°
80°
70°
60°
40°
20°
0°
SEA
NORTH
Baffins Bay
GREENLAND
KAMTSCHATKA
Hudsons Bay
NEW SOUTH WALES
AMERICA
NORTH
NOOTKA
L. of the Woods
CANADA
UNITED STATES
Boston
New York
NEW ALBION
NEW MEXICO
ATLANTIC
TROPIC OF CANCER
SANDWICH ISLES
MEXICO or NEW SPAIN
Caribbean Sea
OCEAN
OCEAN
CHRISTMAS I.
GALLAPAGOS
SOUTH
MARQUESAS
PERU
COUNTRY of AMAZONS
SOUTH AMERICA
FIJI
FRIENDLY IS.
TROPIC OF CAPRICORN
PITCAIRN I.
EASTER I
NORFOLK I.
JUAN FERNANDEZ
MASEFUERO
CHILI
PACIFIC
SOUTH
NEW ZEALAND
ATLANTIC
I. of GEORGIA
ANTIPODES I.
OCEAN
PATAGONIA
FALKLANDS IS.
STATEN LAND
CAPE HORN
OCEAN
ANTARCTIC CIRCLE
OCEAN
180°
150°
120°
90°
60°
30°

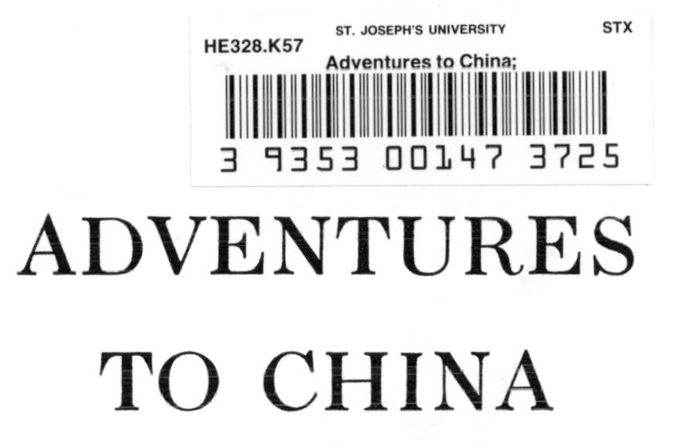

ADVENTURES TO CHINA

Americans in the Southern Oceans

1792-1812

JAMES KIRKER

NEW YORK · OXFORD UNIVERSITY PRESS . 1970

Library of Congress Catalogue Card Number: 78-125507
Printed in the United States of America

To Harold Kirker

Contents

List of Illustrations

Adventures to China

1

The Goal

Before the American Revolution, vessels from the thirteen colonies did not sail eastward beyond Capetown or westward round the stormy Horn. The Indian and Pacific Oceans were closed to the merchantmen of England's possessions; their wealth was the monopoly of the East India Company and the South Sea Company. The merchants of New England and the middle colonies, whose ships ploughed the Atlantic and the seas of Europe, had no personal knowledge of the trade of the Orient. And even though the teas of China figured in one of the early events in their war for independence, only a few American seamen had been to Canton where the green Hyson was purchased in tea chests and the black Bohea was sold in baskets. When final victory in the war with England came to the colonists, the sea routes to China were suddenly open to their merchant ships. The Pacific and Indian Oceans, and the South Atlantic whose waters they join in the high latitudes of the southern hemisphere, became a field of adventure for American sealing and sandalwood vessels bound for China. In search of cargoes to exchange at

Canton, they sailed into uncharted seas and found the way to the edge of the world.

The seal hunters and the sandalwood traders ventured where few had gone before, bestowing the names of their revolution's heroes alike on the cold islands near the Antarctic Circle and the tropical bays of Melanesia and Polynesia. The first American ship's master to hunt seals in the South Pacific considered his commercial adventure a voyage of discovery, promised to keep a journal for President Washington, and to plant the flag where it "hath not yet had accept." [1] The hunters' quest for the southern fur seal took them to almost every island in the path of the great west winds, and along the coast of South America as far north as the Galapagos. Hunting their prey across the Pacific, they learned of the existence of sandalwood in Fiji from an American sailor who guided the first vessel to Sandalwood Island. Its widespread use in the form of incense made sandalwood a far more valuable commodity at Canton than the skin of the fur seal, but the conditions under which sandalwood was acquired—in barter with the cannibals of Fiji—also made it the most dangerous of the adventures to China.

"China," wrote a pioneer sealing captain, "is the first for greatness, riches, and grandeur, of any country ever known." [2] He had participated at Canton in the sale of the second American shipment of seal skins, and then returned home to New England in 1799 to organize his own expedition to the South Pacific. By this time, hundreds of American seamen had visited Canton and some item from the China trader's cargo could be found in most of the dwellings on the Atlantic seaboard from Salem to Richmond. Yet a decade and a half earlier, when independence was gained from England, less than a dozen Americans had actually been to China. One of them, John Ledyard, was among the first to show his countrymen the way to the Orient. Ledyard had met Captain James Cook in London and sailed on the great navigator's last expedition to the Pacific in 1778. Like a number of other seamen on this voyage of discovery, he kept a journal which was surrendered to Cook's successor on orders from the Admiralty, who hoped to prevent any publication prior to the official version. However, a year after the expedition arrived home, an anonymous history of the voyage was published in London and later in Philadelphia. Ledyard returned to America at the end of 1782, deserted his ship while it lay off Long Island, and made his way home to Hartford. There he rewrote his journal, using the anonymously published account as a reference. Ledyard's journal was printed in Connecticut in 1783, the first year the merchants of the new United States were free to undertake a commercial adventure to the Orient.

Ledyard's history of Captain Cook's last voyage emphasized the value of fur skins at the Chinese trading capital of Canton. He recounted how the members of the expedition, reaching Vancouver Island in the spring of 1778, traded with the Indians for fur skins to keep them warm on the cruise they were making in search of the North-West Passage before returning to the island of Hawaii. After the slaying of Captain Cook at Kealakekua Bay early the following year, the expedition again sailed westward in quest of the North-West Passage. Their second attempt brought them in contact with the Russian fur traders on the mainland of Asia, where many of the sailors sold the skins acquired on Vancouver Island for what appeared an excessively high price. But when their vessels lay downriver from Canton six months later, they discovered that the furs they still retained, which had "not cost the purchaser sixpense sterling sold in China for one hundred dollars."[3] The seamen were so eager to return to the Northwest Coast and get more furs that Cook's successor believed his crew close to mutiny.

Shortly after completing his history of Cook's expedition, Ledyard journeyed to Philadelphia to negotiate with the financier Robert Morris for a trading voyage in fur skins to the Northwest Coast and China. "I take the lead," he wrote after several meetings with Morris, "of the greatest commercial enterprise, that has ever been embarked on in this country; and one of the first moment, as it respects the trade of America."[4] However, Ledyard failed to launch the scheme in Philadelphia, and the New York ship whose voyage he later helped promote sailed direct to China, by-passing the fur trade of the Northwest Coast, which was the heart of his plan. And it was seal skins from the Falkland Islands, not sea-otter pelts from Vancouver Island, that comprised the first significant shipment of fur skins carried by an American vessel to the Canton market. Yet Ledyard's boast was partly true, for the vessel sent out under his influence, the *Empress of China,* was the pioneer American ship in the Orient.

The *Empress of China,* Captain John Green, cleared from New York on February 22, 1784. Her departure on Washington's birthday emphasized the patriotic nature of the adventure; Captain Green was released from the Continental Navy expressly to make the historic voyage to China. "Great Number of Inhabetants," recorded her master as the vessel dropped down the Battery, "Salluted us by giveing three Chears which we Returned."[5] The supercargo, Samuel Shaw, was also an officer in the War for Independence. He became the first United States consul at Canton, the only city in China where foreigners were allowed and where their trade and accommodations were restricted to a small area. Shaw sold the vessel's outward cargo to Shykinkoa, one of the dozen or so Canton merchants authorized to trade with foreigners; his name later appears among the papers of the supercargo of another New York vessel as "Shy Fun."[6] The *Empress of China* arrived home in mid-1785 with a cargo of teas and fabrics that brought her owners a return of over 25 per cent on their initial investment. Early the following year, five American vessels cleared for Canton.

Fur skins were not a significant part of the trading commodities in any of the early ventures. When the *Empress of China* cleared from Manhattan on her pioneering voyage, four-fifths of her cargo was in ginseng. The aromatic root of the ginseng herb was extensively used in China; a quarter of an ounce in a cup of tea taken for a few days was considered the elixir of life as well as a cure for practically all the ills that assail mankind. Although native to Manchuria, ginseng was imported on a considerable scale from the New World, where it grew in the mountain regions from Quebec to Georgia. Its Iroquoian name *garentouges* —"human thighs"—has a similar meaning to the "jen-shen" of the Peking dialect.[7] While it was one of the few products the first American traders could profitably send to the Orient, the purser of the *Empress of China* wrote home from Canton: "We brought too much ginseng." [8] The other Western traders also carried it to China, their supply coming first to Europe from the United States. The amount of ginseng offered by the China traders more than doubled, and the price dropped sharply the year the *Empress of China* introduced the "New People," as the Americans were called at Canton, to the Orient.

The second New York vessel to reach Canton, the little sloop *Experiment,* carried an outward cargo that included ginseng and eighteen boxes each containing a thousand "Spanish Milled Dollars." [9] The silver dollar minted in Spain and her American colonies was the standard medium of exchange between the merchants of Canton and the Western traders. The problem for foreigners had always been the one-sided aspect of the trade; the merchants of Europe, and now of the United States, who sought to fill increasing orders for the products of China had almost no exchange commodity. As a result, silver bullion, and very rarely gold, was offered in return for the popular black Bohea and the fine Souchong teas, the varied colored silks and nankeens, and the porcelain demanded in the markets of western Europe and America.

The unerring cargo for a direct voyage to Canton was Spanish dollars; but silver specie was particularly scarce in the new United States. The owners of the sloop *Experiment* included a small shipment of fur skins along with ginseng and their eighteen boxes of Spanish dollars. The skins, mainly squirrel, sold at a loss, but their export indicates that the early merchants were attempting to discover the type of skins in demand at Canton.

"Furs," noted one of the first traders between Canton, Hawaii, and North America, "form the principal and favorite dress of the people of the Northern provinces of China, and those of the rarest kind and highest prices are eagerly purchased by them." [10] The eighteenth-century visitors to the Celestial Empire described the long "vest" or dress of the Chinese which in the northern winters was lined with fur or stuffed with cotton. The quality of the fur depended upon the individual's wealth and position; the coats, neck bands, and caps of the highest orders were lined with sea-otter, while those of a lesser station used the skins of the fur seal and certain land animals. The fur-lined coat was carefully preserved by its owner and sometimes passed from father to son although the usual length of wear was about a dozen years.

Until the published accounts of Captain Cook's last voyage brought the seal hunters of New England and New York to the oceans of the southern hemisphere and the sea-otter traders of Boston to the Northwest Coast of America, the Russians supplied most of the skins for the Chinese market. They operated in a great arc from the Spanish outpost on Vancouver Island to the Aleutians and around the icy Bering Sea to Kamchatka, where the sailors from Cook's expedition sold their fur skins. But their predominance in the rich sea-otter trade was soon disputed by the merchants of Boston who gained a near monopoly of the Northwest fur trade, and the Russians' commerce in seal skins was overwhelmed by the Yankee sealing captains' trading to Canton.* The seal hunters from New England and New York, who searched almost every island in the southern oceans between the Tropic of Capricorn and the Antarctic Circle, brought millions of skins to China in the years between 1792 and 1812.

"Depots of peltry . . ." wrote the historian of the voyage of Étienne Marchand, "give them in return, both teas of which habit has made a want to which perhaps they owe their liberty,

* The term "Yankee" is used to include vessels and crews clearing from ports from Massachusetts Bay to Long Island Sound.

and those rich INDIA goods which republican simplicity scarcely allows of, but which, being necessary to the luxury of EUROPE and her western colonies, become, in the trade of the Americans, articles of barter against commodities of real necessity which Nature has refused to their climate."[11] The sealing and trading captains who sailed with their ladings of skins and sandalwood from the islands of the southern oceans to the mainland of Asia rarely visited the coast of India. They traded almost entirely at Canton for a return cargo made up of for the most part of the dried leaves of the tea shrub. All types of tea come from the same evergreen bush, which grows to a height of three to five feet and has a white flower which resembles that of the wild rose. The difference in teas results from the time of the year the leaves are gathered and the method of curing them. More than half of the cargoes of tea acquired by the Americans were composed of the black Bohea, which was dried at Canton at the beginning of winter. In stating his preference for black Bohea, a Yankee trader at Canton claims that green tea "seduces and enervates the body," adding that a single cup kept him awake all night while a dozen cups of black tea had no effect.[12] The Bohea was sold in baskets to the sealing captains and sandalwood traders and then packed into chests for the long shipment home.

Tea had been imported into Holland early in the seventeenth century and from there spread to the other countries of western Europe. The Dutch introduced the beverage to America a decade before the first tea was imported to England. More than a century later, the hostility of some American colonists to English forms of taxation was expressed in a boycott of tea shipments from England and in the subsequent Boston Tea Party in 1773. Captain John Kendrick of Boston, who brought the second American shipment of fur skins and sandalwood to China, claimed participation in this famous event. He and Captain Simon Metcalf of New York are described by a Connecticut trader at Canton as the first adventurers in fur skins from the

United States.[13] Captain Metcalf was his nation's pioneer in both skins and sandalwood; he carried the initial American shipment of sandalwood and the first cargo of furs—seal skins from the Falklands—to China.

Late in 1784, the year the first American ship sailed for Canton, Captain Benjamin Hussey cleared from Nantucket in the *United States* for the Falkland Islands. He had almost completed a cargo of sea-elephant oil when two English vessels arrived at the Falklands bound on a trading voyage to the Northwest Coast and China. While the vessels were lying at anchor, they were visited by an officer in the tender to the Nantucket ship, and he informed the Englishmen that Captain Hussey had about seven thousand fur seal skins on board which "he had reason to suppose would be disposed of at a moderate price." [14] The two English captains, Nathaniel Portlock and George Dixon, both of whom had served under Captain Cook on his last voyage and knew at first-hand the value of skins at Canton, called upon the New England ship's master and expressed considerable interest in acquiring his skins. As it turned out, Captain Hussey was not willing to sell his seal skins to the English fur traders. Instead, he told Captain Portlock that he intended to go to China himself immediately after his return to America.

Captain Hussey did not go to China with his seal skins as he suggested to Captain Portlock. Yet when he arrived back at Nantucket in the spring of 1786, his vessel carried double the number of pelts originally mentioned for sale to the English fur traders at the Falklands. Thirteen thousand seal skins acquired by the *United States,* recorded the supercargo of a later sealing expedition, were sold in New York for fifty cents apiece and shipped to Calcutta.[15] From Calcutta, the skins were carried to China by Captain Simon Metcalf in the brig *Eleanora* of New York. However, when the *Eleanora* arrived at Macao, the American consul at Canton implied that her lading of seal skins was already stowed before the New York vessel reached India. "With a cargo of furs," wrote Samuel Shaw, "instead of coming directly to China, last season, Captain Metcalf went to the coast of Coromandal, Bengal, and thence to Batavia, and from there to islands in the neighborhood of Macao."[16] The *Eleanora* anchored off the Portuguese colony in August 1788 and shipped her cargo of seal skins upriver to Canton. While waiting for the skins to be sold at Canton, Captain Metcalf's vessel lay among the Wanshan Islands, a dangerous offshore area west of Macao that was outside the protection of either the Chinese or the Portuguese. Here, the *Eleanora* was attacked by pirates, who were beaten off in a battle that took the lives of two officers of the New York brig.

At the time the *Eleanora* sent her seal skins up the Pearl River to Canton, the declining price in ginseng did not indicate a promising future there for the commerce of the United States. One of the four American ships to reach Canton in 1788 disposed of her ginseng at half the price obtained by the *Empress of China* in the initial voyage four years earlier. The basic problem confronting the first American traders to China—shortage of silver dollars due to the depressed state of their home economy—remained unsolved until 1792. In that year, France declared war on England and began the Revolutionary and Napoleonic wars that engaged almost every European nation. The long conflict between the great land power and the great sea power of Europe, and their allies, provided American merchants with the opportunity to become the neutral carriers to the warring nations; and for the next twenty years, until she, too, declared war on England in 1812, the United States sent her ships to trade in most of the ports of the known world. A large share of the commerce of the French and Spanish West Indies and the Dutch East Indies fell to the neutral Americans. Even the British West Indies, closed to the produce of the thirteen colonies after they won independence, were opened by the former mother country.

The improvement in America's economic fortunes was reflected in her trade with China. The problem for American merchants after 1792 was to obtain enough tea to meet foreign as well as domestic demands. In 1803, more than half of the six million pounds of tea carried to the United States from China was re-exported to Europe. The reopening of American trade in the West Indies and a larger share of the neutral trade in Europe made silver bullion readily available for the first time in the United States, and with Spanish dollars available for trade, the main problem for Americans at Canton was ended. The relation between the now solvent national economy and its foreign trade with China appears in a comparison of the export figure for the year the *Empress of China* made the first voyage and that of twenty years later when the war in Europe was at its height. Total exports from the United States in 1784, when one vessel cleared for China, amounted to two million dollars; total exports in 1804, when thirty-one American vessels visited Canton, were seventy-seven million.[17]

After 1792, the leading merchants of New England and the middle states usually sent their vessels on swift, direct runs to China where they purchased cargoes with Spanish silver dollars. The Bostonians were an exception; predominant in the Northwest fur trade, they preferred to acquire their teas and silks with both sea-otter skins and silver dollars. Occasionally, the important mercantile houses designated one of their ships for a sealing adventure or ordered their captains to stop at the islands of the southern hemisphere and obtain skins from the seal hunters who bartered them for provisions and rum. But it was, generally, the lesser merchants of the maritime centers and, particularly, the merchants of the more modest ports from Massachusetts Bay to Long Island Sound who participated in the sealing expeditions which proceeded to Canton. The sealing captains cleared from America without silver dollars or a single item of trade for China; they counted entirely on their luck in finding the far-flung habitats of the southern fur seal.

2

The Hunted

The sealers sought their prey throughout the temperate and colder latitudes of the southern oceans. The southern fur seal was originally found on almost every island in a wide circuit around the globe between the Tropic of Capricorn and the Antarctic Circle. Their breeding grounds ranged eastward from Tierra del Fuego to South Georgia, from the Crozets to the islands of St. Paul and Kerguelen, and from the southern coast of Australia to the mecca of the fur seal at Más Afuera. In the first years after 1792, a vessel sometimes obtained a full cargo of skins at one of the islands and proceeded directly to China after only a few months on its barren confines. But as competition developed, the voyages became longer, covering vast areas in the southern hemisphere and years in time. The orders to a New England sealing captain in 1799 specifically mentioned the Falklands, South Georgia, Island of Amsterdam, and Más Afuera, with instructions to visit "all or either."[1] By this time, a sealing gang might live two or three lonely years on an island of a few square miles; or a single area might hold several hundred men competing for skins.

The first Yankee sealers were led to their hunting grounds by information contained in the published histories of the voyages of exploration in the southern oceans prior to the War for Independence. The captain of one of the initial American sealing expeditions to the Pacific had on board "the latest publications of the English authors." [2] He found the history of Captain George Anson's voyage the most useful source while searching for his prey along the coast of Chile. Included with the text of this famous voyage was a chart of the lower half of South America, where the English navigator records large numbers of seals. Anson rounded the Horn to spend three months at the islands of Juan Fernández, which include Más Afuera, the richest of the Yankee sealing grounds. After describing the thousands of seals on the islands of Juan Fernández, Anson informed the hunters that their prey provided excellent food as well as valuable skins. He notes eating the hair seal "under the denomination of beef" while the fur seal tasted similar to lamb.[3]

The first American sealing captain to hunt at both the Falklands and Más Afuera was influenced in his expedition by reading Bougainville, Hawkesworth, and Cook as well as Anson. English translations of the history of Louis de Bougainville's two voyages, which described vast numbers of seals at the Falklands and contained a detailed chart of the islands, were published in London several decades before the pioneering China-bound New York and New England sealing vessels reached the southern oceans. John Hawkesworth's history of the voyages of Philip Carteret, John Byron, Samuel Wallis, and the first expedition of James Cook was issued in London at the same time. This compilation provided the most complete contemporary description of the seals and their habitats in the southern hemisphere. "The seals," Hawkesworth quoted Carteret from Más Afuera in 1767, "were so numerous, that I verily think if many thousands of them were killed in a night, they would not be missed in the morning." [4] One of the initial Yankee sealing captains in the waters between Chile and Australia credited Carteret with the best description of Más Afuera; another New England ship's master used Carteret's history to reach Pitcairn Island, where, hunting for seals, he discovered the widows and children of the mutineers of the *Bounty*.

Commodore Byron, in the South Atlantic three years before Carteret made his observations from Más Afuera, found the massing of seals on one of the islands of the Falklands so dense it was impossible to traverse certain areas. He set fire to the grass to drive the seals away, a tactic employed by some of the early hunters at the Falklands to concentrate their victims on the more accessible islands. Sailing along the coast of Patagonia in 1764, Byron noted "thousands of seals about the ship." [5] Cook, when he passed the Falklands four years later, also commented on the innumerable seals along the coast of Patagonia; his chart of the Strait of Le Maire showing Staten Island and the southern end of Tierra del Fuego was reproduced in detail in Hawkesworth's history. Like the late eighteenth-century accounts that preceded it, Hawkesworth's history of the voyages of discovery provided good charts of the Tierra del Fuego area but left many of the seal islands of the southern hemisphere uncharted.

The publication in 1777 of the journals of Captain James Cook's second voyage located, for the first time, the principal habitats of the southern fur seal. The great chart bound into the London editions of this work—no editions were printed in the warring American colonies—showed many of the islands later visited by the Yankee sealers. The work also provided a chart of Cook's track from South Georgia, which he rediscovered, to the South Sandwich Islands and suggested the possible location of "Kerguelen's Land," which the American sealers first knew by Cook's designation: the "Island of Desolation." In the text of the journals of his second voyage, Captain Cook noted the concentration of seals from Patagonia to South Georgia and substantiated the earlier accounts of Anson, Bougainville, and Hawkesworth as to the wide distribution of seals in the Falklands-Tierra del Fuego region.

The journals kept by Cook during his third voyage were published in London in 1785 in two volumes, with a third volume completing the history of the expedition by James King, who succeeded to the command after the slaying of Captain Cook on the island of Hawaii. The first American versions were abridgments printed in Philadelphia in 1793 and in New York and in Worcester two years later. One of the early sandalwood traders in Polynesia claims he "read Cook's voyages" as a boy in Maine "in the village schoolhouse." [6] The London editions, with a splendid chart of the world, indicated most of the islands in the oceans of the southern hemisphere visited by American sealers prior to the War of 1812. On his last voyage, Cook located the seal islands along the southern reaches of the Indian Ocean; he designated several of them Prince Edward Isles, named Marion and Crozet after their French discoverers, and charted and called Kerguelen the Island of Desolation. The directions contained in the journals of Cook's last voyage brought a pioneering New York ship from Macao to Kerguelen to hunt seals late in 1792, at the same time the initial China-bound sealing vessels reached the Falklands and the offshore islands of Chile from the mainland of North America.

Several months after the first Yankee hunters landed on the remote island of Kerguelen, a visitor on the island of St. Paul, the nearest land to Kerguelen, recorded the activities of another sealing gang from an American vessel: "They killed the seals as they found them basking in the sun, upon the stones everywhere along the shore." [7] On the rocks and beaches of their breeding grounds in the southern oceans, the seals were helpless before the club-wielding hunters. Their instincts had led them to lonely islands and offshore rocks where they existed by the millions, far removed from predatory land carnivores. The first English historian of Patagonia describes their inaccessible, offshore breeding grounds: "Here are the great herds of sea-wolves and sea lions (such as are described in Lord Anson's Voyage) who sleep on the rocks, and suckle their young in the great caves in them." [8] Thomas Falkner published his history of Patagonia the year before Cook returned from his second voyage, when the seal islands of the southern seas still remained undisturbed by the hunters.

The southern fur seal (*Arctocephalus australis*) and the southern hair seal (*Otaria byronia*) are members of the Otariidae, or "eared seals," which have small pointed ears slanting backwards, covered with fine hair. They spend about half of their life in the sea and half of it on land. "Their situations on rocks or in bays," suggested a member of Cook's first expedition, "have remain'd unmolested since the Creation." [9] However, the Otariidae are actually an offshoot of the bear family and existed entirely on land before they adapted to a seagoing life. The fur "sea bear" has a soft, dense, shiny undercoat which made it the prey pursued almost to extinction by the China-bound Yankee seamen in the two decades before the War of 1812. In dressing seal skins for the home market, the Chinese had developed special skills in separating the long, coarse outer hair from the soft undercoat and in rendering the skin thin and flexible. The southern hair seal—the "sea lion"—had no value at Canton and was never taken as part of the outward cargo for the trade of the Orient. But there was a market for its skin in America and in Europe, and some sealing captains with China their goal hunted both the hair seal and the fur seal.

The male fur seal of the southern hemisphere averages seven or eight feet in length, the female is about one-half the size of her mate. The fur seal is smaller and more agile than the hair seal, and they often share the same sandy shingles and offshore rocks. The adult male's fur is dark brown, sometimes almost black, with a scattering of white hair about the head, neck, and anterior portions; the full-grown female is silver gray, although the older ones have dark brown sides and backs. "They have the finest eyes imaginable," wrote an early observer at the Falklands, "and there is no fierceness in their countenance: I remarked that when they were expiring their eyes changed colour, and their crystalline lens became of an admirable green." [10] When the first hunters came ashore, their prey were without apprehension of danger; the seals lay tranquilly along the sandy stretches and rocks while their nearest neighbors were killed and skinned. Soon, however, they became wary of the hunter, relying on their acute senses of hearing and smell for protection. "Even in sleep," noted the head of a sealing gang in the Indian Ocean, "something warns them of danger and they precipitate themselves into the sea." [11] But their only real defense was to find a new breeding ground on more distant and inaccessible rocks and beaches.

The creation, and maintenance, of a harem is the occupation of the polygamous Otariidae during the rutting season. The older males—"wigs" as they were designated by the hunters of the late eighteenth century because of the curly hair on their heads—are the first to arrive at the breeding grounds. They take places close to the water which they hope to maintain against all competitors until the arrival of the females. The battles for best places commence as soon as the front row is filled and more males haul themselves up from the surf onto the rocks or beaches. Despite their original strength and vigor, the early arrivals are often driven back as they are forced to battle against fresh contestants. The struggle for first place along the water's edge is intensified by the arrival of the females, those along the front line struggling to keep their superior places from the competitors pressing from the rear.

The battle-scarred wigs welcome the females—"clapmatches" as the early sealers called them—from their stations nearest the water.[12] They bow and are solicitous to a particular female until they maneuver between her and the sea and she cannot escape; then she is driven to a place in the harem. Shortly after their arrival on the breeding ground, the females give birth to the young they have been carrying from the previous year—usually only one pup—who weighs about six pounds and has a coat of black fur. The most successful wigs gather a harem of twelve to fifteen females, although their station is subject to constant invasion by their competitors in the rows behind them; the less able males content themselves with one or two clapmatches. Captain Cook, who made the latter observation off Patagonia in 1775, noted, also, the "superannuated" wigs "lying growling in a retired place, alone."[13] The wigs never leave their harems until the rutting season ends; during their long vigil on land, they exist entirely on the fat of their bodies. When they return to the water, they are shadows of their former selves.

The early Yankee hunters knew almost nothing about the seals of the southern oceans. Their principal authority, Captain Cook, supplied the most complete contemporary description of the habitats of their prey, but he did not always distinguish between the fur and hair seals in his accounts of their breeding grounds and their habits. The future sealing captain Edmund Fanning describes one of the initial expeditions to the Falklands in 1792 when neither he nor the ship's master knew anything about the seals they set out to kill and skin. Fanning and his gang selected as their first victims a group of three hundred hair sea lions which they mistook for fur sea bears. With a loud shout, he recounts, they raised their clubs and marched upon the rookery: "This noise alarmed the lions, so that they immediately rose, and sent forth a roar that appeared to shake the very rocks on which we stood, and in turn advancing upon us in double quick time, without any regard to our person, knocked every man of us down with as much ease as if we had been pipe stems."[14] Fanning had read in the histories of the English explorers how the fur seal stands firm and submits to death when separated from the water by his hunter but did not know that the hair seal breaks for the sea when attacked.

Actually, both species attempt to defend their harem when faced by predators on the shores of their breeding grounds. The smaller fur seal is less capable of resistance, but he tries to protect himself and his family by biting and snapping. "Self," recorded a Connecticut seaman on Más Afuera in 1798, "got badly wounded by a seal." Writing from the same place and under the same month a year later, he noted: "2 Hands bit by seals today." [15] The more powerful hair seal generally makes an initial stand against the enemy but then breaks for the water, followed by his harem. The hunters sometimes used a gun to destroy the large male hair seals; an early visitor to the Falklands described the death of a sea lion from gun-shot: "One of those which were mortally wounded, in his last struggles seized some of the cornflags that surrounded him, tore them in pieces with his teeth, and scattered them about; but without bellowing or making any noise." [16] When Edmund Fanning and his crew became more familiar with the habits of the two different species of the southern Otariidae, they used a gun or lance against the male hair seal although the club was adequate for the destruction of the female and her pups.

A wooden club or stick was the weapon always used against the smaller fur seal. The usual procedure was for the hunters to form a line between the seals and the water, destroying their prey as the line advanced inland. The slaughter was methodical although not always dispassionate. "What with the roaring of the seals, maddened to desperation," wrote a New England greenhand of his first hunting experience, "and the yelping of the young pups, together with the shouts of the crew, formed to my mind, a kind of pandemonium scene, from which I should have been exceedingly glad to have escaped." [17] The hunters struck the seal on the nose with a stick three to six feet long. The blow merely stunned the seal, reducing it to an inactive state. When as many of their prey as possible were knocked down in a certain area, the seals were killed by a stab in the breast and skinned on the spot.

A visitor on the island of St. Paul in 1793 described a gang from a Boston vessel skinning fur seals: "As the skins alone were their object, they left the carcases on the ground to putrefy at leisure, strewed in such numbers as to render it difficult to avoid treading on them in walking along. A shocking spectacle was thus exhibited at every step, while the smell infected the atmosphere around."[18] The skin was taken off rapidly with the blubber adhering to it, which made it easier to beam. It was laid on a slab and the blubber cleanly removed with a beaming knife. The skin was then washed, the flipper holes sewed up, and carried to the pegging ground. The pegging ground was located as close as possible to the slaughtering area, but had to be fairly level and free of stones and rocks. Each skin was stretched out with ten pegs and a single clear day sufficed to dry them sufficiently for stacking. The skins were stacked on shore and allowed to sweat before stowed for the China market; or they were stacked in caves until the ship returned to the island to pick up the men and the cargo. If the expedition was also taking hair skins, the work of killing and skinning was similar, except that the beamed and washed skin was rubbed with salt and packed away for the American and European market.

"Hitherto," noted the historian of Marchand's voyage to the Pacific, "the Americans act more then they write."[19] He was commenting, in 1801, on the scarcity of printed material relating to the activities of the Yankee fur hunters and traders bound to China. The New England and New York sealing captains and officers did not share their knowledge or experience among their fraternity; they maintained a close secrecy concerning their adventures. The nature of the occupation favored concealment rather than dissemination of information relating to the habitats or habits of their prey. The slaughter of the fur seals by even a single crew was enormous once a breeding ground was discovered. And if other ships arrived, either by accident or through information, the field was rapidly destroyed for all. The sealing vessel *Catherine* cleared from Manhattan in 1803 in search of the Crozet Islands, which Cook had located and charted on his last voyage, but her destination was given simply as "Canton." The absence of information in the marine columns of the newspapers concerning sealing expeditions contrasts sharply with the detailed accounts of voyages to Europe and to the East and West Indies. But discoveries could not be kept secret indefinitely, and before the *Catherine* returned home with her cargo of tea and silk, a New England vessel had also found the way to the Crozets.

The more famous sealing areas were never secret, but the first hunters there attempted to discourage later arrivals with false information. The supercargo of a New Haven vessel reaching the Falklands early in 1797 consulted with the two Yankee sealing captains already there on the habitats and numbers of their prey; one said he obtained only six hundred skins in four months of labor, although the other, on the point of departing, admitted taking twenty thousand skins in eight months of hunting. If misinformation proved unpersuasive, the gang already established on the hunting ground supplied the newcomers with rum until they could no longer work or admitted the field belonged to the initial arrivals. Acknowledging that "a glass of grog will get a sailor over to your side anytime," the leader of a Salem gang resorted to force to make his drunken men hunt in competition with rivals from another Massachusetts vessel who preceded them to the offshore islands of Chile.[20] Force, however, was usually directed against the rivals. The captain of a Boston sealing adventure on the southern coast of Australia took such violent measures in his battles with competitors that the governor of the neighboring English penal colony of New South Wales wrote home for instructions on dealing with the American hunters so "pernicious to the public interest." [21]

Yet the hunted were extraordinarily bountiful to the hunter. The southern fur seal provided American seamen with much more than the millions of skins for the Canton market. The hunters made suits out of seal skins for warmth and shaped moccasins from them for comfort; they sewed the furs together for blankets and stretched skins across the openings and roofs of their stone or wood huts. The flesh of the seal saved many isolated or shipwrecked sealers from starvation; for once a gang established camp on the desolate breeding ground they relied largely upon the meat of their prey. Whether the meat was roasted, fried, broiled, or stewed, the hunters often preferred the flesh of the seal to that of lamb or beef. Seal's tongue "when salted, affords no despicable resource in a scarcity of provisions"; while for soup the flippers were considered superior to the green turtle, which the men gathered in great numbers at the Galapagos Islands on their way to China.[22] One shipwrecked sealer, Daniel Foss, lived for five years entirely on the meat of the southern Otariidae. Cast ashore, alone, on an island only one-half mile long and barren of wood, he cut the meat in strips with his knife and dried it by the hot mid-day sun. The salt deposited in the rocks by the sea was used to preserve his only source of food. Fortunately for him, the faithful seals returned regularly to his tiny island.

3

The Hunters

The proper crew for a sealing voyage was described by Captain Amasa Delano as comprising between twenty and thirty men, at least a third of them experienced hunters. This was never achieved, notably so in the case of Captain Delano himself. Hunting among the offshore islands of Chile in 1804 with a ship's company composed largely of convicts smuggled on board at New South Wales, he maintained discipline by giving his greenhands "good wholesome floggings." [1] The Yankee sealing adventures in the two decades that preceded the War of 1812 departed with inexperienced crews and, sometimes, inexperienced captains. The New York ship's master who led the second expedition to the Falklands in 1792 claimed a knowledge of sealing, but when the vessel reached her destination and he designated sea lions as fur seals, it was clear he was new at the business. Almost ten years later, in the heyday of hunting on Más Afuera, the supercargo of a Salem expedition wrote from the Southeastern Pacific: "Our people . . . all green hands at the business." [2] Sealing voyages with Canton as their goal were long and unpredictable and the occupation arduous and depressing. Once safely home, the hunter was generally disinclined to repeat his lonely and dangerous task.

Most of the sealing crews came from the farming communities adjacent to the New England seaports from which the majority of vessels cleared. The crews on ships belonging to New York were also often recruited in the New England ports from Nantucket Sound to Long Island Sound. The master of the *Betsey* of New York, bound for the seal islands of the southern oceans in 1797, selected his crew from Stonington and New Haven; the Manhattan mercantile house of Gouverneur and Kemble designated the *Maryland* for a sealing voyage the same year and ordered her to New Bedford, where the ship's company was recruited. The town of Hudson was the only New York community that supplied sealing crews largely from within its own territory. Founded in 1783 by seafarers from Nantucket, this new maritime village, enlarged by more settlers from their island home and the neighboring Martha's Vineyard, entered the sealing trade shortly after the initial expedition to the Falklands. Situated more than a hundred miles up the Hudson from Manhattan, the river town provided the majority of sealers from the state of New York.

The New York owners of the *Maryland* specified that their sealing crew selected in Massachusetts "be natural born subjects of this country." [3] But such a requirement was rarely imposed or fulfilled; the danger of impressment of seamen by British men-of-war scarcely existed in the remote parts of the world visited by the sealers and the sandalwood traders. Englishmen, Scotsmen, and Irishmen were repeatedly hired as officers and seamen on American sealing and sandalwood voyages, either at the port of clearance or anywhere along the voyage to Canton and back. Furthermore, the year the *Maryland* sailed for the hunting grounds of the Southeastern Pacific was only a decade after the establishment of a federal government in the United States; the connection between the former colonies and the mother country was not then completely severed. A New England seaman who kept a journal of the *Asia's* sealing and oil expedition to the Indian Ocean in 1792 described himself: "Silvanus Crosby is My Name and English is my Nation Nantucket is My Dwelling Place and Christ is My Salvation." [4] The Yankee mariner's sense of a complete separation from England was more a manifestation of the War of 1812 than of the post-colonial age.

Most of the greenhands who shipped on sealing voyages bound to China hoped to take up farming when they returned home to New England or New York. They did not aspire to be professional sailors. Captain Charles Barnard of Hudson opened the account of his sealing expedition to the Falkland Islands with the quotation: "The mariner not vainly brave/Combats the storm and rides the wave/ To rest at last on shore." [5] For the Yankee seal hunter, this usually meant a single voyage, although the expedition often involved years in time and half the globe in space. However, in this time and space, the seal hunter was not merely a sailor. Much of the expedition took place on lonely islands where the business of sealing—killing, skinning, stacking, and waiting—engaged the seamen in activities different from that of the usual sailor. But when the course of the expedition cast him back more fully in the role of sailor, on shore leave for example, the New York and New England greenhand generally followed the pattern of the seamen of old England. Commenting on how a young New Haven sealer spent most of his money at Canton on liquor, the supercargo of the vessel adds: "He, however, among the rest, calculates to be a farmer." [6]

While most of the greenhands were boys or young men off the farm, or in a few cases on leave from college, some women are recorded among the ship's company of expeditions to the southern oceans. "One of the crew," noted the narrator of a Nantucket sealing and whaling voyage to the South Atlantic in 1800, "a disguised female; had been two voyages undetected." [7] There is no information as to how the impersonation was maintained, but another Massachusetts female sailor, Lucy Brewer, told how she escaped discovery during several years sea duty in the War of 1812. She wound a bandage across her breasts and wore a tight pair of trousers, which were removed only "with great precaution." [8] Lucy Brewer claimed she enlisted as a marine on the *Constitution* and took part in the capture of the *Guerriere* off the coast of Nova Scotia. Watching this battle from the other side was another alleged female sailor, Almira Paul, who purportedly entered the British navy to avenge the death of her husband in an engagement with a Yankee privateer. She claimed to have served on several British and American ships before retiring from the sea in 1814. Almira Paul described herself as "always garbed in my pea jacket and trowsers," although she stowed her female attire in her sea chest in case of detection.[9]

It was possible for the young seamen who shipped on sealing adventures to return home from a single voyage with enough money to purchase a farm or start a small business. Unlike ordinary sailors who relied on wages, the members of a sealing expedition shipped on shares and profited directly from the sale of the skins at Canton. This explains the intense competition between rival sealing gangs on the hunting grounds and the violence and deception that often accompanied the rivalry. As a rule, half of the shares in the adventure were reserved for the owners and half for the crew: one quarter for the officers and one quarter for the ship's company. A share was generally defined as one skin in every one hundred of the total skins taken by the expedition. In a few cases, a flat sum of five or six dollars per man for each one thousand skins, collected jointly by the gang, was paid rather than a specific share. The captain advanced his crew a quarter of their share in cash at Canton to invest in goods for themselves or in the company's purchases. The remaining three-quarters of the sealer's share, computed on the sale of skins in China, was paid after the vessel returned to the home port.

"A sailor's share," wrote the supercargo of the *Neptune* from Canton in 1798, "is upwards of twelve hundred dollars, and most of them are calculating to turn farmers." [10] But his expedition was unusually profitable; the ship's company in Yankee sealing adventures averaged between a half or a fourth of this sum. The master of a New York brig, which competed with the *Neptune* for skins at both the Falklands and Más Afuera and reached the Orient at the same time, estimated his and the crew's total share on the basis of the sale of their cargo in China: Captain, $2160; first officer, $1000; second officer, $960; carpenter and steward (each), $600; cooper, $480; blacksmith, $360; ten crew members got between $240 and $120 apiece, plus a share in $420 to be divided among "deserving" members of the ship's company.[11] The crew of a Massachusetts vessel that completed an equally successful sealing adventure at Canton a decade later received almost the same shares in dollars when they returned to New England as those quoted above for the New York brig in 1798.

The investment of their cash advance at Canton—a quarter of their full share—was the most common way for the future farmers to increase their earnings. This sum was available to them for use at the Chinese trading capital for their own private commercial adventure; the rest of their share was paid at the home port in America. If they did not want to trade privately with the merchants of "China Street" in Canton, the ship's master invested their share in the company's goods. When the Connecticut crew assembled at the Manhattan house of the captain of the *Betsey* at the completion of their voyage in 1799, each man who had not traded for himself at Canton received an "adventure bundle" consisting of a bolt of nankeen, a packet of handkerchiefs, and two pieces of silk. The goods acquired in China by the hunters, carried back to New York or New England in their sea chests or freight, free with the company's merchandise, sold at home for at least double the original cash outlay.

Occasionally, the sealer carried money with him from America to invest at Canton and managed to keep it intact during the long outward voyage. A nineteen-year-old New Haven youth took nine hundred dollars with him when he shipped as a greenhand on one of the numerous vessels named "Betsey" in the sealing trade. With his future private adventure at Canton in mind, he departed from the home wharf with a huge sea chest, twice the size of an ordinary one. The roof of the forecastle had to be pried off to lower the chest below; but it provided adequate stowage for his personal purchases at Canton, which resold in Connecticut for several thousand dollars. However, few hunters set out on sealing adventures with such large sums of money. If they carried any at all, it was only enough to purchase a bit of china ware or a piece of silk on commission for a neighbor or for a member of their family. A much more usual way for the future farmer to increase his earnings was to remain on the sealing ground and continue the hunt after his vessel departed for Canton and home. When the first Connecticut ship arrived at Más Afuera, she was greeted by seven hunters left there from the initial New York vessel to reach the seal island direct from America. The Connecticut ship took the seven hunters from New York and their skins on board when she sailed for China, leaving on the island her own gang of eleven men with the agreement to be picked up by another ship in twenty months. The terms between the master of a Boston vessel and a crew of nine men who also remained on Más Afuera were fifteen dollars per man per one thousand skins; an agreement signed between the captain of another Boston vessel and a sealing gang of four men left on the lonely island of St. Paul specified fifty dollars for the gang for every thousand skins taken over a period of two years.

The master of a sealing vessel received far more benefits than his share in the sale of the cargo of skins in China. Whether or not he was paid a salary, the captain was always given the privilege of a specified number of tons in the ship's stowage for his own purchases at Canton, an important privilege since the real profits of the voyage were derived from the sale in America or Europe of the return cargo from China. The captain often owned a part of the vessel itself and shared directly with the other holders in the adventure in the net profits from the voyage. Edmund Fanning, an officer on three sealing adventures prior to the War of 1812, was captain and part-owner of the vessel on the last two voyages. Captain Amasa Delano tells of his family's share and labor in a sealing adventure in which the vessel *Perseverance* and her tender *Pilgrim* were owned by them and half a dozen men in the vicinity of their native town of Roxbury: "Many were the perils and dangers we three brothers encountered in this long, extraordinary and tedious voyage. We built both the vessels we were in ourselves and navigated them two and three times round the globe." [12] Another New Englander, Mayhew Folger, first served in the South Pacific as master of a sealing vessel owned by two Salem merchants, but he returned in 1807 as part-owner of the *Topaz* on the voyage that discovered the mutineers' colony on Pitcairn Island.

The other officer who benefited generously in the profits of the voyage was the supercargo. In the numerous cases when he was a part-owner in the adventure or a son of the owner, his profits often exceeded the captain's. At least half of the sealing and sandalwood adventures carried a supercargo, whose position in respect to the captain was not so rigidly defined as on a straight passage from America to China. The long and indirect voyage, the indeterminate character of the seal hunt, and the dangers of the sandalwood trade did not favor a precise division of authority. The owners of the *Huron* ordered the master and supercargo to consult together and attempt to agree, otherwise "the captain's opinion should yield"; the supercargo overrode the master when the vessel was hunting off Chile and turned a losing voyage into a successful one.[13] The supercargo always transacted the business at Canton, sometimes was ordered to take command of the ship if the master died or was incapacitated, and, in the case of the *Jenny* of Boston, given authority to decide whether to divert the ship's sealing activities to sandalwood trading.

The physician on the *Sally* of New Haven—"Bound on a Sealing voyage to the South Seas"—received two shares in the expedition.[14] But like most doctors on a sealing voyage, he took an active part in the land operations on the hunting ground, for his expectations depended on the number of skins taken to Canton. The physician on the *Neptune,* also out of New Haven, was placed in charge of the expedition's pegging grounds at the Falklands, becoming an expert in his task of drying skins. He also accompanied the hunters in the killing and skinning activites; on one of his early ventures, he killed one hundred and twenty seals, reporting in his journal: "Like Sealing well." [15] He worked hard as a sealer, although he had been sick most of the outward voyage and relied extensively on the captain for medical attention. When the captain bled him, the doctor wrote that recovery was impossible; the captain, in turn, had little confidence in the physician, allowing him to set a broken arm only after a violent dispute as to the proper method. Both survived; in fact, the physician later elected to remain on a South Pacific island in charge of the sealing gang while the ship went on to China and home to New England.

The American agent at Canton for a number of sealing adventures described the proper ship for the trade as about two hundred tons burden and copper-bottomed. This was, actually, the average tonnage of the vessels sealing in the southern oceans. Individually, the ships varied considerably in tonnage, size of crew, and armament. Two successful expeditions departed from the seal island of Más Afuera for Canton within several months of each other in 1798: one vessel, ninety tons burden, carried a crew of twenty-four; the other, three hundred and fifty tons burden, had a crew of thirty-five. The smaller brig departed from New York without any heavy armament; the larger ship cleared from Connecticut with twenty twelve-pound guns. But on the way to Canton, the small brig narrowly escaped capture by natives at the Marquessas Islands and her captain then ordered the carpenter to make false wooden guns, which were mounted at the portholes. Although a number of small sealing vessels were similarly armed with wooden guns, which the men called Quakers, the larger vessels usually mounted guns as well as carrying small arms and boarding pikes. "I was powder-monkey for the two guns aft on the starboard side," wrote a New England mariner about himself when he was a ten-year-old boy on a sealing adventure in 1800, "and was much pleased when the drum beat to quarters." [16] His father commanded the *Sally*, a vessel of two hundred and forty tons armed with twenty guns, on an expedition to the island of South Georgia.

Americans hunting along the east coast of South America in the vicinity of the Falklands had little need for armaments, but when they pursued their prey among the offshore islands of Chile and Peru, they were subject to attack by pirates or privateers or to bombardment from the Spanish coastal fortifications. The hazardous areas in the passage from the seal islands to Canton were the pirate-infested Java Sea and the South China Sea. Yet in the actual execution of their trade on remote and uninhabited islands of the southern oceans, the sealers were relatively safe from natives, pirates, or privateers. The situation changed when the sealers discovered the existence of sandalwood at Fiji and decided to make the fragrant heartwood of this tree a commodity in their adventures to China. The need for armament was established after the initial attempt to trade, when the pioneering vessel lost half her crew in a massacre at Tongatabu before even reaching the Fiji Islands.

Many months were spent on the outward voyage to the sandalwood and seal islands of the southern seas. The sandalwood vessel *Eliza* reached the equator from Salem "after A long and tedious Passage of Sixty-Eight days." [17] She had by-passed the Cape Verdes, although most of the vessels stopped there for provisions. Lying off the west coast of Africa below the Tropic of Cancer, the islands supplied pigs, goats, chickens, pumpkins, watermelons, oranges, bananas, and eggs. Provisions were often more available there through a barter in used clothes than an exchange of money. And many a greenhand sealer who relinquished a jacket, shirt, or trousers for a bottle of rum regretted the transaction when his vessel reached the colder environs of the hunting grounds. Large quantities of salt were purchased at the Cape Verdes to preserve the cargoes taken on the islands close to the Antarctic Circle where the fur skins could not be properly pegged and dried and to preserve the hair seal skins that some of the China-bound expeditions hunted for the American and European market.

The vessels usually took four to five months to reach the Falklands from their port of clearance and at least several more months to make the islands of the Southeastern Pacific and Australasia. The amount of time spent on the hunting grounds depended mainly upon the quantity of the prey, the number of the competitors, and the vessel's opportunity for other forms of trade; occasionally, it depended upon shipwrecks, privateers, desertions, and even the integrity of the ship's master. Once the cargo for Canton was stowed, the vessels struck out for the mainland of Asia, although they usually broke the passage with a stopover at the Hawaiian Islands for refreshment and provisions. The last lap of the outward voyage brought the vessels to rest at Whampoa, twenty miles downriver from Canton. The vessels lay there from one to three months before their sails were set for the far-off American homeland. "This is a fourth birthday of mine since I left N York," noted the head of a sealing gang as he finally began the homeward passage from China.[18]

The long journey gave the crews, if inclined, plenty of time for studying, reading, and writing. The supercargo of a Connecticut vessel held classes in seamanship whenever the weather permitted during a three-year voyage to Canton and back; a young seaman from the same state traded his daily ration of rum to an older seal hunter for lessons in practical navigation; another New England youth taught an "old tar" how to read in return for daily lessons in seamanship. Many of the greenhands carried books in their sea chests which were either lent among the crew or acquired by them on the death of the original owner. A Massachusetts youth who shipped on the *Dromo*'s sealing and trading expedition to the Pacific took along a dozen books, including titles on navigation, arithmetic, and geography. He died early on the voyage and in the auction of his belongings, another greenhand bought one of the arithmetic books for $2.30. When he, too, died, the book was sold for $2.00; but the second purchaser also died on the voyage, and the book changed hands for a third time among the crew at a final price of $1.75.[19]

A number of officers and seamen kept journals of their hunting and trading expeditions. "Stole away to write," confided a Yankee sailor whose ship carried sandalwood to Canton in 1812.[20] Their journals are sometimes described as logs although there is considerable difference between the two. The log of a sailing vessel in the late eighteenth and early nineteenth centuries was kept every one or two hours, when the ship's speed and course were recorded along with the winds and a brief description of the weather. While they were not always kept with the same regularity of logs, the journals reveal a more detailed and personal history of the voyage. "I a poor fellow," wrote the supercargo of a Salem sealing vessel during a storm in the South Pacific, "seting down in the cabin, with all dead lights lashed in, writeing with a nasty lamp which pitches way every minute, & oils me all over."[21] Continued during the land operations, the journals record the lonely and arduous life on the hunting grounds and the danger and excitement of the sandalwood trade.

4

The South Atlantic

Far from the hunters' homeland, in the course of the west winds, lie the seal islands of the South Atlantic. Those that yielded the richest harvest of furs—the Falklands, Staten Island, and South Georgia—were all visited by the first China-bound sealing vessels to hunt the southern waters of the Atlantic. The pioneering adventure was led by Captain Daniel Greene in 1792 in the *Nancy* of New Haven, and carried a sister ship, the *Polly*, which lay off South Georgia while Captain Greene hunted a thousand miles westward at the Falklands and Staten Island. After acquiring cargoes at their respective hunting grounds, the two vessels kept a rendezvous, where the skins taken by the sister ship were discharged to the *Nancy*, which Captain Greene sailed to China. Captain Greene returned to the South Atlantic in 1797 and hunted among the Falklands and the offshore islands of Patagonia for a year, stowing about fifty thousand skins. However, he did not then sail direct to the Orient as on his first adventure; instead, he completed his cargo for Canton on the island of Más Afuera in the Southeastern Pacific.

A dozen China-trading vessels out of New England and New York followed the *Nancy's* lead to the South Atlantic in the decade after her initial sealing adventure in 1792. About half of the vessels acquired a full cargo of skins among the offshore islands of the Falklands, Patagonia, Tierra del Fuego, and the snow-covered island of South Georgia; the other half duplicated Captain Greene's second voyage, relying on the island of Más Afuera to complete their ladings for Canton. A number of other Yankee captains hunted the South Atlantic during this, and the following, decade. However, after obtaining cargoes that included sea-elephant and whale oil as well as fur seal and hair seal skins, they returned to their home ports; they did not cross the Cape or round the Horn to trade at China. In the decade after 1802, a few of the Yankee vessels bound for the seal islands of the Southeastern Pacific tarried briefly at the Falklands, but their prey was scarce by this time and none seriously attempted to hunt there between 1806 and the voyage of the *Nanina* in 1812.

Captain Charles Barnard of Hudson brought the *Nanina* to the Falklands with orders to remain until a full lading of skins was obtained for the Canton market although the southern fur seal was then practically extinct in this area. Shortly after arriving, he heard from an American vessel that a state of war existed between the United States and England. He left the western islands frequented by British whalers and sailed around to the less visited eastern islands, where he discovered the wreck of a ship bound from New South Wales to London, with fifty people from the vessel camping on the shore. Captain Barnard, by informing them of the war between his and their country, sealed the doom of the *Nanina*. Leaving his vessel at anchor in the bay, he went off with a few men in a small boat to kill wild hogs on a neighboring island as provisions for the shipwrecked English. But they seized his vessel during the mission of good will and sailed away. The sealing captain from Hudson and his four companions were stranded at the Falklands for two years before an English whaler rescued them and carried them to the coast of Chile.

From there, Captain Barnard made his way to Más Afuera, where he was finally picked up by a New York ship bound for China. "After an absence of four years and seven months," he writes, "I had returned without a shilling in my pocket." [1]

The fur trader Peter Corney visited the Falklands in 1814, the year Captain Barnard was rescued by the British whaler. He describes the Yankee hunter's vegetable gardens overrun with weeds and a town deserted by the Spanish, reminders of the two different groups of people who periodically inhabited the islands in the years between the first American sealing expedition and the War of 1812. The islands had initially been claimed for France by Louis de Bougainville in 1764 when he founded a settlement on the largest island, East Falkland. A year later, Commodore John Byron established a settlement on the other large island, West Falkland, claiming the entire area for England. Several years later, France sent Bougainville back to the Falklands to deliver the territory to Spain, who also claimed it. After accepting the Falklands from France, Spain transported a small colony there from Buenos Aires; this included two priests "who, beholding their settlement, were overwhelmed with grief." [2] The rugged, wind-swept terrain appeared bleak and inhospitable to the Spaniards. The Yankee sealers, in contrast, found the mountains and promontories "some of the grandest seans that can be conceived of, precipices 200 feet high, exactly perpendicular, looks more like work of art than of Nature, below you see the sea breaking & dashing against the bottom." [3]

The Falkland Islands were covered with a strange form of vegetation, the tussock, or Penguin-Grass, which provided a natural fodder for the herds of wild goats and hogs that roamed the islands, as well as a nesting place for the Magellan penguin and the fur seal. One of the first chroniclers of the Falklands, stumbling upon a herd of seals in the tussock, describes the resulting noise as "resembling the grunting of hogs, the bellowing of bulls, the roaring of lions, succeeded by a sound like the blowing of the largest pipes of an organ." [4] The sealers used the tussock to make a temporary hut when they were occupied on the shore or as a shelter if caught on land during a storm. But the reed-like tussock could not serve as fuel, and the absence of wood at the Falklands was the main disadvantage to an otherwise excellent provisioning place for vessels hunting seals or bound to and from the Pacific Ocean.

The outer, western islands were the principal sealing area in the Falklands for the China-trading vessels from New York and New England in the decade after 1792. The hunters' area comprised an arc radiating from Port Egmont about fifty miles northwest to the Jason Islands and an equal distance southwest to Swan Island. The islands included in the arc lay on the windward side of West Falkland, stretching in the direction of Patagonia and Staten Island, which were also included in the sealers' hunting grounds. The other South Atlantic hunting area, the island of South Georgia, was a thousand miles eastward across the ocean on the fringe of the Antarctic. The mariners of this period designated West Falkland the English Maloon, as opposed to the larger Spanish Maloon, or East Falkland, the ninety-mile-long island occupied by the garrison from Argentina. Fortunately for the American hunters on the neighboring English Maloon, the Spaniards had little interest in sealing.

Arriving at the English Maloon after the four- to five-month passage from America, the sealing vessel anchored at Port Egmont or at one of the protected harbors on Swan Island, West Point Island, or New Island. The vessel remained at the anchorage, for strong rip tides and sudden squalls made navigation among the offshore islands, where the prey was hunted, dangerous except by small boats. From the anchorage, the sealing expedition constructed a sloop, or shallop, to transport men and supplies to the hunting grounds on the outer isles and to bring the skins to the pegging area, which was located on the nearest land available to the vessel. The frame of the shallop was usually carried on shipboard to the Falklands and launched from the anchorage within a month's time after arrival; if only the timber

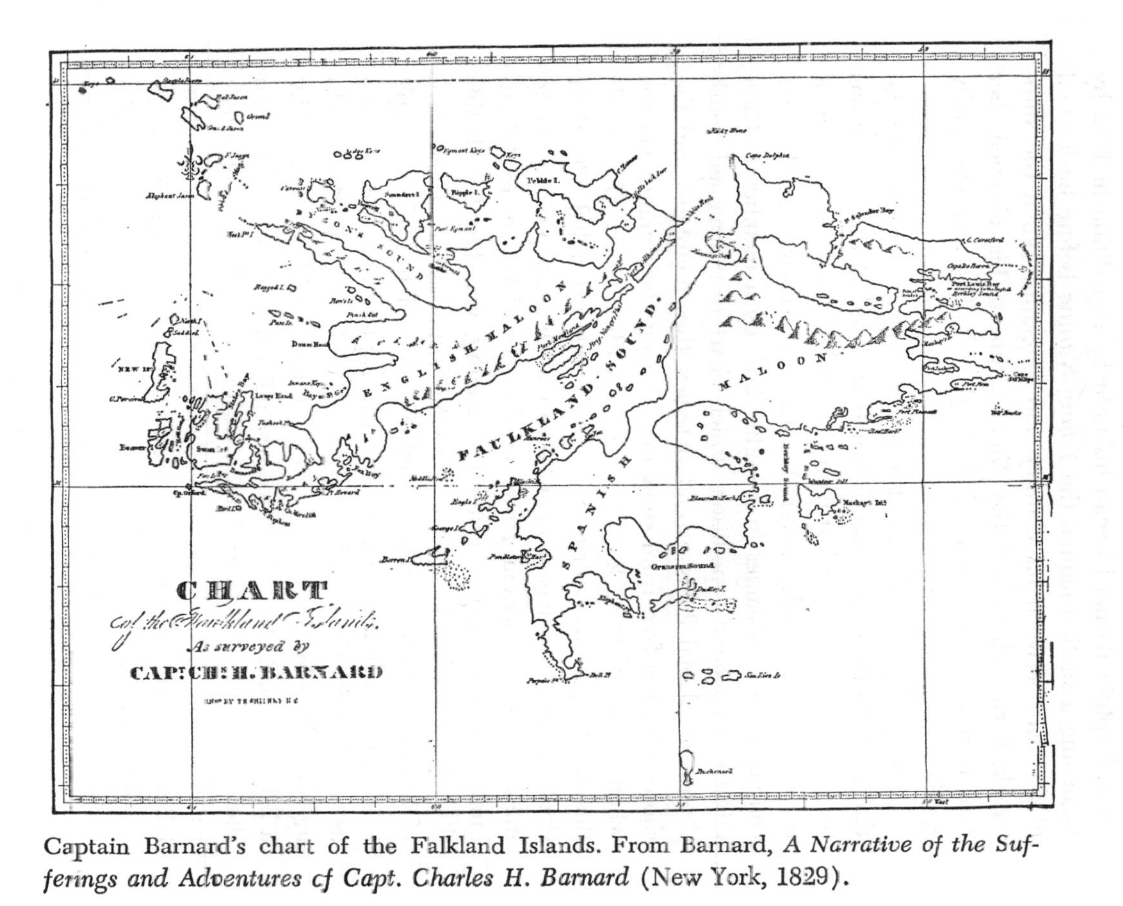

Captain Barnard's chart of the Falkland Islands. From Barnard, *A Narrative of the Sufferings and Adventures cf Capt. Charles H. Barnard* (New York, 1829).

was brought from home, the shallop took several months to complete. Captain Barnard began his unlucky expedition in 1812 by launching a shallop named the *Young Nanina* before he learned of the war between his country and England. When the shipwrecked English seized the *Nanina* during his absence, her American crew were set adrift in the shallop and eventually reached Buenos Aires.

The shallop was also used in the sealing excursions from the Falklands to Patagonia and Staten Island and in the expeditions to South Georgia. The last-named island consists of a chain of mountains perpetually covered with snow, their ragged peaks compared to the "flames in a raging fire" by a member of Captain Cook's second expedition, which charted and named South Georgia.[5] Glacial fields extend between the mountains and the shore, which is free from snow only during the summer months when the land at sea level is covered with tussock. The vessels that reached South Georgia from the Falklands sailed with their shallops; no ship's master planned to launch a sloop there during the short hunting season. However, the second Yankee captain to hunt at South Georgia, Edmund Fanning, was faced with this difficult task when he gained the sealer's anchorage at the close of winter in 1800. Captain Fanning expected to find the ship's tender, which had been sent ahead to explore and was to serve as a shallop for the expedition. Instead, he found only the wreckage of the tender; later, he learned the men had been rescued by a British ship. As the winter ice was not yet broken up along the shore, his crew built their shallop with material from the tender's wreckage on an iceberg "notwithstanding the almost constant falling of the heavy winter snows on us."[6] Captain Fanning's shallop was finished by the time the seals hauled out of the water, and he carried away almost sixty thousand of their skins to Canton.

After the vessels arrived at the Falklands, only a few men remained at the anchorage to construct or finish the shallop. The rest of the crew were formed into gangs to work on the hunting grounds, and whatever small boats the vessel possessed were used until the shallop was completed. A New Haven "rawhand" who shipped on one of the first China-bound expeditions to the South Atlantic recorded a typical sealing excursion from the anchorage at West Falkland to the outer islands: A gang of eighteen hands departed at dawn in the shallop for the seal isles where they killed, skinned, and washed about eight hundred, after which "supper tasted good." The next day, they killed, skinned, and washed thirteen hundred. They killed five hundred seals on the morning of the third day, but the afternoon and the following two days were occupied with beaming skins and sewing up flipper holes. The shallop, which returned to the anchorage after depositing the gang, arrived back at the hunting ground several days later and took off the beamed skins. The hunters remained on the outer isles for two weeks before returning to the vessel for a short respite. But in less than a week's time, they were transported back to the hunting ground, where they killed nine hundred seals the first day, "the handsomest skins yet taken." And another cycle began, similar in detail and results to the preceding one.[7]

The strenuous work of the sealing gangs at West Falkland was performed under difficult weather conditions. The outer isles lie in an exposed situation, swept by heavy seas and strong gales which often prevented the shallop from landing provisions. "June 21—Nothing but Seal to eat," recorded the New Haven rawhand from the outer islands in 1797, "and out of Provisions. June 28—Shallop and Mates Boat arrived with provisions. Plenty to eat and Drink. July 4—Saw the Shallop trying to get to us blowing a gale from NE she bore away . . . not much to eat and Nothing to Drink Independence Day with us. July 9, 10, 11, 12 —Nothing but Bread to eat. July 13—Shallop Came With the Boat & great joy we got everything on board and sailed for the Cove." But after a few days rest at the anchorage, the gang was hunting again, on the outermost island: "July 20—Blowing a gale with steady rain. Nothing to eat and no house to sleep in. Wet thru and chiled with cold." [8]

At the same time most of the ship's company and officers were hunting in gangs on the outer islands and rocks, a few members of the crew least likely to excel at killing and skinning were stationed on the pegging ground to receive the skins as they were brought back in the shallop. The pegging ground was located on the mainland of the English Maloon, or West Falkland, adjacent to the good places of anchorage. The ship's doctor on one of the early voyages was placed in charge of this phase of operations after he helped finish the shallop. He and several men cleared the tussock from an area suitable for pegging skins, cut a path to the shore, and then built themselves a "little cottage" of tussock. The men received the skins as they were landed from the shallop, dried and shaped each one with the aid of ten pegs driven into the ground, and stacked and aired the cured skins. One man could peg four hundred skins in a day. During the time the skins were pegged to the ground, they were continually turned and scraped to remove the blubber left on them by the sealing gangs. The skins were taken from the pegs when cured and stacked for transportation in the shallop to the vessel, where they were stowed for the Canton market.

One clear, bright day was sufficient for curing a skin. Such days, however, are rare in the Falklands. The skins were often kept in pegs for one to three weeks before they were cured and ready to be stacked. The conditions for pegging and curing skins at Staten Island and Patagonia were similar to those at the Falklands. The Yankee hunting area at Patagonia comprised the offshore rocks and islets as far north as Deseado, the Port Desire of the sealers' logs and journals. The skins were pegged and cured farther south on a stretch of ground known as the "New Haven Green" because of its frequent use by vessels out of that port. This area along the coast of Patagonia was also used to cure skins by some of the expeditions that hunted at South Georgia, where the severity of the climate and the brevity of the sealing season—from the end of November to the beginning of February—excluded the long pegging and drying process. The sealers' anchorage at Willis Island, on the northern tip of South Georgia, was a stormy and gloomy one compared to the protected bays of West Falkland. Even the seals seemed more hostile: "The youngest cubs barked at us," wrote one of the first visitors to the island, "and ran after our heels when we joassed by, trying to bite our legs." [9] The South Georgia skins had to be salted first, and later dried at Patagonia or along the coast of Chile.

Work on the pegging ground at the Falklands was determined by the weather and the regularity with which the shallop conveyed the skins from the outer islands. The few men living on the pegging area were more comfortable than the ship's officers and hands killing and skinning on the seal islands. Although their hut of tussock was not always waterproof, they were snug enough on rainy days when no pegging could be done and they remained indoors. The ship's doctor, who was in charge of the *Neptune*'s pegging ground, recorded the quiet activities of such days, which included mending his clothes, brewing his own "maiden-weed" tea, and making a flannel shirt which "troubled me some to put the sleeves in." Sometimes, late on a wet afternoon, he went off with his gun and shot ducks and geese. And when the next day, too, proved a stormy one, he "stayed in & cooked 1 goose and 2 ducks exceeding good." [10] Like the gangs on the seal islands, the men on the pegging ground were supplied by the shallop with provisions from the ship. But if high seas and winds prevented the shallop or small boats from landing, they had the mainland behind for foraging and were not restricted to eating the meat of seals as were their shipmates laboring on the outer islands. Foxes and rats provided the most troublesome conditions at the pegging area, continually destroying the provisions and the skins.

If the expedition carried a supercargo, he was often left in charge of the ship at the anchorage while most of the crew hunted in gangs and a few men tended skins on the pegging ground. The supercargo on the *Neptune,* one of the most profitable sealing adventures out of New Haven, performed this task at the Falklands with only the company of a dog and a cat. And as both the steward and the cabin boy were out on the islands slaughtering the prey, he did his own washing and ironing and tended a vegetable garden. The solitary watchman on a New York vessel at the West Falklands anchorage recorded his "several good dinners of potatoes, cabbage & lettuce all of my own planting with turnips & raddishes." [11] These and other vegetables —onions, spinach, and celery—provided an important supplement to the sailors' fare. The watchmen at the anchorage also went inland from their gardens and picked wild berries, which were stewed on shipboard for puddings or distributed raw to the crew to mix with their pancakes. The watchmen on the vessels that lay at the South Georgia anchorage did not have the gardening or berrying diversions available at the Falklands. However, Captain Nathaniel Storer's ten-year-old son, who remained on the *Sally* at the South Georgia anchorage, recorded his own particular sport of "running on sea-elephants' backs . . . where these animals lay in rows on the beach." [12]

The sealers hunting the outer islands at the Falklands were provisioned by the shallop from the ship's store as regularly as the weather permitted. Their usual victuals were beef, pork, bread, molasses, tea, coffee, and rum. They used the blubber of seals for cooking fuel, which made them "nearly as black as negroes." [13] When storms isolated the gang on the hunting ground from the vessel, meat from the ship's store was the most dispensable item as the seal provided a substitute. But the men did not like to go without their daily ration of bread or the molasses they used to sweeten their coffee, for they were "much attached to what they call slops, which is tea and coffee, in this cold uncheerful country." And "there was always a terrible clatter at breakfast and supper by the crew with their tin pots, beating up eggs as a substitute for milk in their tea and pea coffee."[14] The eggs of the penguin and the albatross were used also in place of flour, an item in constant demand for the sealers' pancakes.

Innumerable eggs were gathered at the Falkland rookeries, the rows of mud nests about a foot high occupied by the albatross and the penguin, the latter called "jumping jacks" by the hunters. One of the early mariners at West Falkland describes the "general stillness" that prevailed at the rookeries when the seamen first began gathering eggs and the birds regarded them with curiosity rather than fear. "Here, during the breeding season," he writes, "we were presented with a sight which conveyed a most dreary, and, I may say, awful idea of the desertion of these islands by the human species."[15] But as the plunder of the nests at the rookeries began to match the slaughter of the seals on the rocks, the birds offered resistance. Then, the seamen had to pry the birds off their nests with sealing clubs before they could collect their eggs. The penguin and albatross retaliated by pecking at hands and ankles, which caused much pain to their predators but did not prevent the depletion of the eggs; one sealing gang stacked over ten thousand in a single day. Immersed in seal oil and packed in layers of sand in casks, the eggs kept fresh from four to six months and could be eaten long after the vessel departed for China or the seal islands of the Pacific.

The hunters gathered clams, mussels, and limpets at low tide, but fish was scarce at the Falklands. Wild fowl was a more available substitute for salt pork or seal meat, the crews preferring the geese of the upland to those of the lowland. The taste of the upland geese, who fed on berries, is described by a member of Bougainville's expedition as "exquisite, either boiled, roasted, or fricasseed."[16] The lowland geese fed on shell fish and had a "fishy" taste. But they were far more numerous and accessible, swarming in vast flocks along the water's edge, where the seamen killed them with oars and boat hooks. They [illegible] killed the rooks, although not for their flesh. "The Falkland I[illegible]" noted a

Yankee captain who made two expeditions to the islands, "is, unquestionably, the most knowing, mischievous, and saucy bird among the feathered race; and gives to the way-worn sailor much vexatious trouble, during their hunting and sealing excursions."[17] The rook followed every move the sealers made, and if any article—knife, cap, mitten, jacket, powder horn, pot—was left unguarded, it was carried away in their sharp claws or beaks. Captain Barnard of the captured *Nanina* called them "flying monkeys," recounting the misery they brought to his abandonment on Swan Island, stealing his supply of eggs and trying to take the moccasins off his feet while he slept.

The wild hogs and goats that roamed the English Maloon and the smaller western islands were hunted for food. The pursuit of the boar provided the sailors with a sport both exciting and practical, although many ugly wounds resulted and a number of the ship's dogs were lost in these encounters. Dogs left on the islands by the sealers, or by the whalers who used the area for watering and refitting, ran wild among the tussock. Captain Greene left one of the *Nancy's* dogs behind at the Falklands when he sailed in 1794 on the passage that initiated the direct run from the South Atlantic hunting grounds to Canton; he found the animal when he returned to the islands on his second expedition in the *Neptune*. Captain Barnard considered the theft of his dog by other sealers one of the most painful episodes in the two years he was marooned on West Falkland after the English seized his vessel. During this time, he built a stone hut with a skin roof and lived on the meat of seals, hogs, goats, and fowl and on eggs and berries.

The hunters at the Falklands spent their respite from the rain and wind-swept seal islets at the anchorage. They made suits, hats, and moccasins out of seal skins, cut wooden pins for the pegging ground, and made candles from the tallow of the wild goats. They held sham elections with themselves as candidates on the days that corresponded to such political events at home; the crew of one vessel, according to the supercargo, electing "the very opposite in every thing to what I hope and believe they have got in Connecticut."[18] Sometimes the sailors drank too much rum and were confined to "Drunken Island" near the anchorage at New Island. Or, if another American vessel was in the vicinity, dances were held on shipboard. The doctor who tended the pegging ground tells how he left his tussock hut and went down to the anchorage to attend a "ball on board, music was flute, drum, and violin."[19] Another dance was held several days later, just before one of the ships departed for a sealing excursion to Patagonia.

The vessels that made their anchorage at West Falkland hunted both the southern coast of Patagonia and Staten Island. Captain Greene reached Staten Island from the English Maloon on the pioneering sealing adventure from the South Atlantic to China. A Boston ship's master, Benjamin Lee, had actually preceded him to Staten Island, but he did not go on to Canton with his seal skins. "Adieu inhospitable country," wrote Captain Lee in 1793 as he headed his vessel back to her home port. "May snow, rocks and marine animals be in future thy only companions."[20] Yet, shortly after he left the anchorage at Squally Cove, the Yankee sealing vessels in the South Atlantic began to hunt the wild coast of Staten Island. Situated off the eastern tip of Tierra del Fuega, the island has a mountainous terrain covered with forests and a climate similar to the Falklands. A New England sealer described the abundant shell fish and sea fowl at Staten Island and the "tart red berry the size of a wild cherry" and the "delicious white berry the size of a junipor" which made an excellent tea.[21] His was one of three vessels owned by a group of merchants from the Connecticut inland town of Norwich that hunted at Staten Island in 1800; the vessels were later confiscated by the Spanish while completing their China cargoes among the seal islands of the Southeastern Pacific.

Although the Spanish disregarded the Americans at the lonely Falklands and Staten Island, they kept a close watch for them on the coast of Patagonia, particularly in the vicinity of

Deseado. "The Island of Seal looked very tempting" recorded the supercargo of a New England vessel off Port Desire in 1797; a few days later his gang was threatened with imprisonment and driven off the island by the Spaniards.[22] Officially, all foreign trade with Spain's American possessions was illegal and entrance into her colonial ports admissible only under conditions of distress. But when the sealing captain had something to trade which the commandant at Patagonia wanted, an agreement was reached enabling the Yankees to hunt the offshore islands for a limited time. However, the largest portions of seal skins acquired in Patagonia were purchased from the natives by barter. The Patagonians had a culture in which the seal played a prominent role; they lived in huts covered with seal skins, were clothed from the same source, and relied largely upon the seal for meat. They traded their skins for alcohol, tobacco, and old clothes.

The crews from sealing vessels lying off Patagonia traded with the natives for guanaco blankets and the meat of the guanaco which they compared with deer. The natives also introduced them to other kinds of meat: the wild cat, the ostrich, and the tiger. They bartered armadillos with the Yankees, who attempted to preserve them, after death, to take back as curiosities to their New York and New England homes. The Patagonians particularly liked the biscuits the seamen had among their rations and traded for this item with horses; twelve biscuits bought a horse, one biscuit bought a day's rental. "Set a sailor on horseback," quotes an American sealing officer at Patagonia at the close of the eighteenth century, "and he will ride to the devil." [23] Whenever his men had a holiday, they raced their horses up and down the grassy slopes. Some of the hunters at Port Desire at this time told of seeing a young Englishman the Spanish had bought from the Patagonians who held him a prisoner for six years, having taken him when he was an eleven-year-old cabin boy on his father's ship.

The time spent at Patagonia was often one of relative ease after the strenuous months of seal hunting on the outer islands of West Falkland or at the remote island of South Georgia. The *Hope* of New Haven tarried three months at Patagonia late in 1800, trading with the natives and drying her skins taken at South Georgia. Then, after beating along Tierra del Fuego for two months without getting past the Horn, her master turned the vessel in the opposite direction and reached the Orient by the eastern passage. Shortly afterwards, the captain of the *Diana* of New York lost a month trying to take his ship into the Pacific before he, too, set a course for China by way of the Indian Ocean. But while many of the vessels that hunted in the South Atlantic rounded the Horn to complete their cargoes at the seal islands of the South Pacific, those who reached China by the eastern passage did not stop at the seal islands of the Indian Ocean. "Sighted St. Paul's" is the day's entry in a journal kept aboard the *Diana* for 5 June 1801 as she sailed across the Indian Ocean toward the Sunda Strait. Her master did not know that a crew from a Boston vessel was hunting the desolate island of St. Paul nor that the head of the gang had been involved there for almost a decade in a strange sealing adventure.

5

The Indian Ocean

The islands of St. Paul and Amsterdam were the first seal haunts in the Indian Ocean to be visited by the Yankee hunters. Situated midway between the Cape of Good Hope and the coast of Australia, they were known to the mariners sailing the eastern passage to the Orient. The Americans generally reversed the names of the two islands in their ships' logs and journals, following the example of many of the English navigators, although Captain Cook placed them accurately on the charts of his voyages and retained the original Dutch designation of Amsterdam for the northern island and St. Paul for its neighbor sixty miles southward. An account of the islands supplied by the master of the London ship *Mercury* in 1789 describes "the seals innumerable" on the island of St. Paul, which he calls Amsterdam.[1] Another member of the *Mercury*'s fur trading expedition, who published his own history of the voyage, suggested: "It would perhaps answer very well if a vessel were fitted out to the Island of Amsterdam to collect seal skins." [2] By the time his account appeared in print, two New England sealing vessels, one bound for

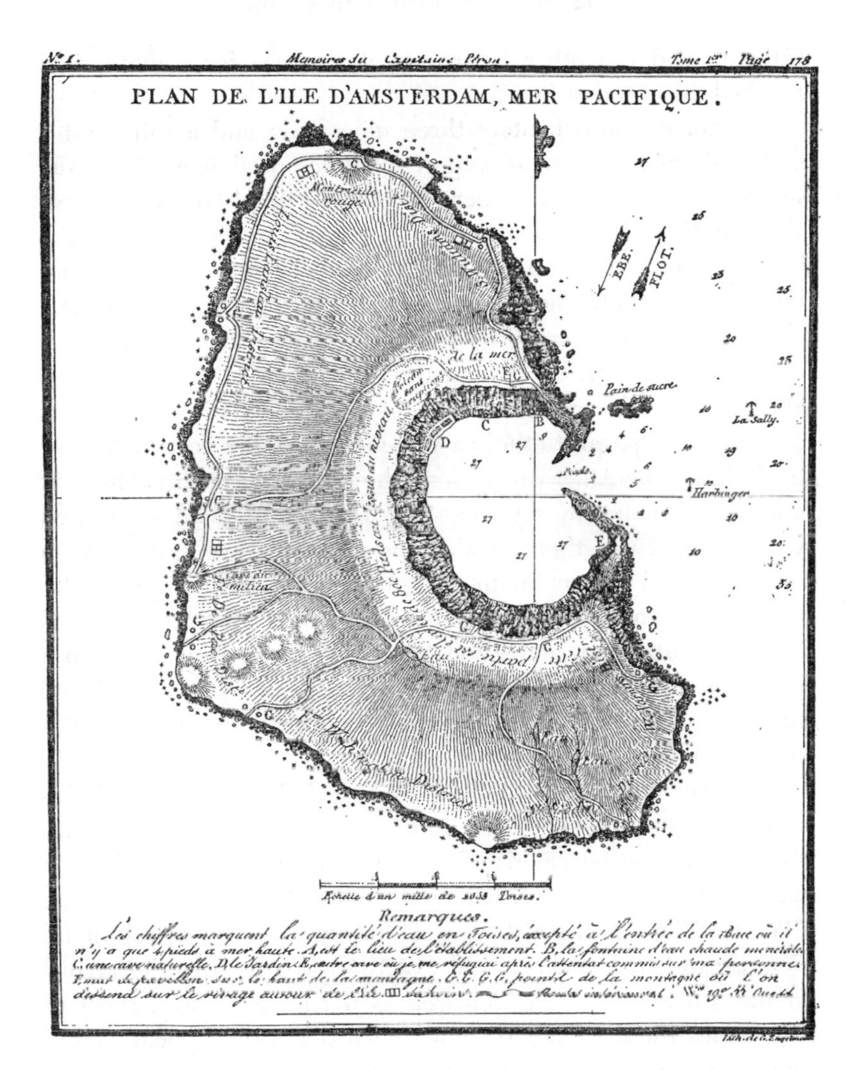

Captain Péron's chart of the Island of St. Paul, showing the *Sally's* anchorage. From Péron, *Memoires Du Capitaine Péron, Sur Ses Voyages* (Paris, 1824).

Calcutta and the other in search of a cargo for Canton, had reached the island of St. Paul.

St. Paul is approximately three miles long and a mile and a half wide and rises in elevation eight hundred feet above the sea. One of the early sealers compared the island's elliptical shape to that of the ear of a man, the crater in the center of the island corresponding to the concha of the ear. St. Paul is iron-bound except on the northeastern side, where the headlands meet at a narrow inlet flowing from the sea to the crater. The crater was inaccessible when Willem de Vlaming described the island at the end of the seventeenth century; the causeway forming the crater's rim adjacent to the sea was more than five feet high. Fortunately for the American sealers, the sea had broken through in a shallow channel by the time they reached St. Paul a hundred years later. It was then possible for a gang to live and work on the island and still maintain communication by small boats with their vessel anchored outside the channel. The neighboring island of Amsterdam, about twice the size of St. Paul and also a habitat of the southern fur seal, was much less frequently visited since its rugged coast rises precipitously above the sea without a safe anchorage.

The volcanic island of St. Paul revealed a strange and disturbing nature to the Yankee hunters. Fires smoldering beneath the surface emitted clouds of smoke by day; while at night, the flames were visible at great heights along the island's silhouette. "The land," wrote the historian of the expedition in search of La Pérouse which passed St. Paul exactly one year after the arrival of the Americans, "then appeared as if covered with a sheet of fire, whilst the illuminated smoke gave that vivid appearance to the sky which generally portends a hurricane." [3] Fire and its effects shaped the character of the island. The rocks were scarred and black, and the sandy beaches the color of gunpowder. The hunters' shoes sank deep into the spongy soil formed by the decomposition of lava; their passage between the sealing stations was long and fatiguing. Some parts of the island, where the scorching ground bubbled beneath the surface, could not be traversed; in other areas, the soil was covered with moss from which erupted streams of vapor and smoke. The boiling water formed brackish springs surrounded by tall grass similar to the tussock the sealers found at the Falklands.

The crater was the heart of the island. Originally a great lake of fire, it provided the sealers with a safe harbor for their small boats, which gained the haven by crossing a bar separating it from the stormy sea. The first hunters lived in a hut with a thatch roof at the "Town Point" on the northern end of the crater, where they built a pier designated "the American Wharf." [4] They chose this site because it was adjacent to the island's only good source of drinking water, a warm stream which they used for cooking. The seals also lived along the crater's rim, lying on the rocks and in the tall grass. The water in the crater provided the hunters with a variety of fish, almost the only native food available to them except for the blue petrel. The sealers snared the "night bird," as they called the petrel, with flaming torches that attracted the birds in their nocturnal flight. The albatross, belonging to the same order as the petrel, was a frequent visitor to the island of St. Paul. But while one species of the petrel was known to the seamen as a harbinger of trouble, the albatross was considered a bird of good omen. It was not killed for food by the hunters on St. Paul but served them as a scavenger, devouring the carcasses of the seals strewn about the rocks and beaches.

Half a dozen New England sealing vessels with Canton as their goal hunted the island of St. Paul in the period between 1792 and the War of 1812. The first hunters from America actually reached St. Paul in 1791, but their vessel, the *Warren* of Newport, had Calcutta as her destination; it was not until the following year that a vessel flying the American flag gained the island with the intention of obtaining a cargo of fur seal skins for the Canton market. When the hunters from the *Warren* landed off the channel, they found the rim of the crater a solid mass of seals. They also found that the rich hunting area was already under attack by a gang of English and Chinese sailors from a vessel operating out of Macao under the Prussian flag, which was one way British traders in the Orient attempted to evade the monopoly of the East India Company. A truce was arranged between Captain Jacob Smith of the *Warren* and his English rival and was maintained as long as the two vessels remained anchored outside the channel to the crater. However, vessels could not lie off St. Paul's hunting ground until their cargoes were completed as they did at the Falkland Islands. The crater provided small boats with a safe landing place for men and supplies and a loading station for skins, but the general calm over the inland crater—"smooth as a pond" noted a visitor in 1793—did not prevail elsewhere on the island's periphery or along the neighboring Amsterdam's ironbound coast.[5] The two islands, separated from the nearest land masses by thousands of miles, lie on a vast, rolling surface of unhindered wind and waves. After landing their gangs and supplies on St. Paul, the vessels sailed away in search of other seal islands or trading areas.

Shortly after the Rhode Island vessel and her English rival departed, the effects of competition between the men remaining on the island erupted in quarrels and threats of violence. The two gangs worked the area around the crater in hostile proximity for about four months until the English and Chinese sealers suddenly disappeared. But St. Paul is a small place, really only a single mountain whose steeply rising slopes encircle the crater on three sides, and the head of the New England gang soon discovered his rivals sealing on the other side of the mountain. The Yankees constructed a house nearby and renewed the competition in the new area. However, they kept their headquarters at the Town Point, and they continued to use their original location as the expedition's pegging ground. The crew across the mountain was supplied every three or four days from the hut on the crater's edge; the skins were carried back on the return trip to the pegging area. Only one man remained on the pegging ground, pinning down the skins as they arrived and overhauling the ones already stacked. The lone watchman on the crater's edge stayed inside the hut during the frequent periods of rain, making wooden pegs and mending clothes. When the rain and wind lessened, he caught fish in the crater or searched for mollusks along the rocky entrance to the channel.

The hunters isolated on the inhospitable island of St. Paul remained badly in need of provisions once their original supply was exhausted. Very infrequently, a passing vessel anchored off the inlet and traded provisions for seal skins while taking on a supply of fish from the crater. The first Yankee sealing adventure at St. Paul was supplied after ten months on the island with bread, liquor, rice, coffee, trousers, and skinning knives from an English vessel trading out of India. The members of the second expedition to St. Paul in an American vessel, the *Emily*, were less fortunate in their dealings with visiting ships. The *Emily*'s sealing crew of half a dozen American and French sailors had been on the island eight months when an English warship anchored off the channel and her officers and men came ashore. The sealing captain took the officers on a tour of the island while the warship's crew, armed with a supply of rum, bargained with the members of the sealing gang for skins. The trading commenced orderly, but when the hunters "tasted the rum in sufficient quantity to affect their understanding, they lessened the heaps of skins with a profusion that knew no bounds." [6] The sealing master returned to find his storehouse knocked down and almost a thousand of his own skins gone.

A combined American-French adventure, the *Emily* was fitted out at Mauritius and sailed under the Stars and Stripes. The continual warfare between France and England made it exceedingly dangerous for a vessel in the Indian Ocean or the China Sea to hoist the flag of the French Republic. Although the *Emily* was commanded by a New Englander, her expedition to St. Paul was actually led by a Frenchman, Captain Péron, who was in charge of the small sealing gang that planned to remain on the island for fifteen months while their ship made a trading voyage to the Orient. Arriving at St. Paul in mid-1792, they found the crew from the *Warren* of Newport gone although their English and Chinese rivals were still hunting around the crater and over the mountain. As Péron knew little about sealing, he applied to the other ship, which had returned for its gang, for an experienced hand. His request was answered by an American sailor whom the master of the English ship out of Macao was eager to discharge. Péron's gang included another American—an ex-British seaman sailing out of Boston—and two French sailors.

The *Emily's* sealing crew were soon involved among themselves in a conflict in which sides were drawn on a basis of nationalism. The two Americans succeeded in obtaining all the armaments, seriously wounded Captain Péron, and drove the two other Frenchmen from the hut the hunters occupied together at the northern end of the basin. This was the house abandoned by the initial American sealers from the *Warren* and is described by a visitor as a "small miserable hut, as dirty and offensive as that of an Hottentot; and it was surrounded on every side by the dead carcases of seals and sea-lions." [7] After living in banishment for a number of days in a cave on the opposite side of the crater, Péron managed to regain the armaments. The feat was accomplished with the aid of one of the French sailors who pretended to change his allegiance and returned to the community house to watch for a time when the Americans relaxed their guard. Five days passed before the opportunity came and the signal given for Péron and the other banished sailor to subdue the Americans. The death of one of the Frenchmen evened the sides and the seal hunters lived on the island in a repressed state of hostility for three years before their leader was rescued. During this time, the sealing captain attempted to remain alone as much as possible, experiencing "little charm in the society of the grosser men." [8] He found consolation in the books he brought to the island, in his crayons, and his flute.

Captain Péron said his gang's violent behavior was influenced more by their fear of abandonment than their greed for seal skins. Abandonment, or the possibility of it, overshadowed every expedition to St. Paul and Amsterdam. The half-dozen New England ship's masters who landed gangs on the islands sailed from their dangerous shore as quickly as possible to hunt other sealing grounds or trade on the southern coast of Australia, the Northwest Coast of America, or at Canton. There was always a chance the ship would not return. The intermittent war between England and France presented many hazards to neutral shipping, while the nature of the trading ventures in the distant areas of the Pacific often prevented a captain, even with the best intentions, from returning for his hunters at the appointed time. Captain Péron's suspicion that the *Emily* was not going to return to St. Paul to pick up his sealing crew actually created the situation that led to their abandonment. Under the influence of this fear, he disclosed the vessel's mixed nationality to the commander of the English warship who made the one-day visit to the island during which the sealers were robbed of their skins. The British warship fell in with the American-French vessel off the China coast and captured her as a prize. Péron was finally rescued at the end of 1795 by a ship bound to the English penal colony at New South Wales. Although offered passage only on the rescue vessel, and not stowage for his three thousand skins, Péron was so anxious to get off the island, he left behind the labor of more than three years.

A month after Péron's departure, Captain Ebenezer Dorr brought the *Otter* to St. Paul. A member of a Boston family active in the early fur and sandalwood trade to China, Dorr expected to find the sealing gang left on the islands of St. Paul and Amsterdam two years earlier by his family's ship *Fairy*. Finding the sealers gone, he took possession of all the skins he could locate, including those belonging to Péron. Yet he failed to discover ten thousand skins the men from his family's ship had hidden in caves along the crater's edge. Dorr then sailed for New South Wales, reaching Port Jackson one day after Péron landed from the

London ship that rescued him. When the Frenchman demanded the return of his skins, the Bostonian acknowledged his claim but insisted on keeping them for sale in Canton as surety against his carrying charges. However, he offered Péron the berth of first officer on the *Otter,* now bound for the Northwest Coast and China. The French sealing captain accepted, not wishing to be separated, again, from his skins. Dorr and Péron traded on the Northwest Coast before bringing the *Otter* to Monterey, where she was the first American ship to visit California. They then sailed to the Orient where the vessel discharged a mixed lading of skins and loaded a cargo of teas, silks, and porcelains for New England.

Captain Péron was not successful in his attempts at Canton to get payment from Captain Dorr for his skins taken off the island of St. Paul in the *Otter.* He reached Boston in another ship at the beginning of 1798 and remained there for more than a year, engaged in a lawsuit against Captain Dorr; he describes the time spent in New England as the happiest in his life. With the money he obtained in his lawsuit, Péron outfitted the *Sally* in Boston for a second sealing voyage to the island of St Paul. Because of hostilities between France and England, the French sealer again designated a Boston mariner, Captain Stephen Hall —"my pupil and my friend"—the "titular" master of the vessel.[9] Péron, also as in his earlier adventure in the Indian Ocean, commanded the sealing crew on St. Paul while the New England captain took the vessel to Canton.

Arriving at the hunting ground in 1800, Péron found one of the sealers from his old gang still there. The French sailor was now employed by the Dorr family to collect the ten thousand skins overlooked by the captain of the *Otter.* Péron also found seven stranded sealers from the Dorr's sloop *Nancy* which had reached the islands two years earlier and was wrecked off the coast of Amsterdam after landing a sealing gang. The first assistance for the shipwrecked sealers came a year after their vessel was lost when another Boston fur trader arrived at St. Paul and displayed considerable interest in their situation. The Boston trader visited the islands several times during the next six months, relieving the stranded hunters of over twelve thousand skins. By the time Péron arrived in the spring of 1800, the last of their seal skins were taken on shipboard and the trading vessel then headed for Canton with the *Nancy's* ex-sealing master and two of his men.

The Dorr family had asked Captains Hall and Péron to supply the stranded men on St. Paul with provisions, but their request was not heeded. On the contrary, Péron hired the five remaining sailors from the wrecked vessel for his own sealing gang, as well as one other seaman from the first rescue ship sent out by the owners of the *Nancy*. The presence of the rescue vessel merely increased the friction between the Dorrs and the stranded hunters on St. Paul; for when the sealers failed to follow the example of their captain and depart from the island on the owners' terms, they were denied provisions from the rescue ship. The situation was complicated as the captain had failed to make a written contract with the hunters before the loss of his ship on the rocks off Amsterdam and exercised no control over their sealing activities on the island of St. Paul where they took refuge after the wreck. Sullivan Dorr, considering the situation from the owner's point of view, described the men as "a mass of corruption." [10] Another family ship, with William Dorr supercargo, was also dispatched to the island of St. Paul with instuctions to at least try to retrieve some of the skins. But she tarried at the Falklands, unsucessfully hunting seals, then turned into the Pacific to try her luck at Más Afuera.

Captain Péron and his recruits hunted on St. Paul for over a year. During this time, Captain Hall took the *Sally* to Canton, returning to the island in mid-1801. He anchored the vessel outside the channel entrance to the crater; Péron was waiting on the shore. "Mr. Hall," wrote the Frenchman, "impatient to fly into my arms, threw himself into the dinghy; before reaching the bar, the dinghy was stopped by the first waves; it was tossed upright and capsized; my unhappy friend was swallowed up, and disappeared forever."[11] Péron, who sailed from the island shortly after the death of Captain Hall, commanded the last significant expedition on St. Paul. His departure closed the decade of sealing begun there by the initial New England hunters in the *Warren*. After ten years of slaughter along the shore of the crater and among the rocks on the leeward side of the island, the fur seals of St. Paul were practically extinct.

In the year after the first Yankee hunters reached St. Paul, Captain Simon Metcalf of New York brought the *Eleanora* to the island of Kerguelen on the stormy edge of the Indian Ocean. Situated a thousand miles southwest of St. Paul, the island was discovered several decades earlier by Yves de Kerguelen, who led an expedition in search of the elusive southern continent, the legendary Gonneville Land of French explorations. Kerguelen described the remote and inhospitable island as "Southern France"; Captain Cook visited it on his last voyage and called it, "with great propriety," the Island of Desolation.[12] Cook sailed around the island, disproving Kerguelen's claim that it was part of a great southern continent and suitable for colonization. Cook's description of the numerous "sea bears" on the rocks around the island led Captain Metcalf to Kerguelen from the French colony at Mauritius—more commonly called the Isle of France by the Americans—which lay in the track of most vessels sailing westward from Asia. Captain Metcalf had reached Mauritius from China and was trading at the French colony at the same time Captain Péron was organizing his unlucky expedition to the island of St. Paul in the *Emily*.

Captain Metcalf was a pioneer in the sealing and sandalwood trade; he carried the first shipment of seal skins from America to the Orient in 1788 and the first shipment of sandalwood from Hawaii to Canton several years later. At the end of 1792 he brought the adventurous brig *Eleanora* on the first American expedition to Kerguelen, anchoring in the bay Captain Cook named Christmas Harbor, at the northern end of the island. Using the directions contained in the journals of Cook's last voyage, the New York sealing captain located the bottle which the great English navigator had buried on the north side of Christmas Harbor. A member of Kerguelen's expedition of 1771 had originally fastened the bottle, with a note inside, to a projecting rock overhanging the bay. Cook found the bottle four years later, wrote across the back of the note, deposited a silver twopenny piece, and placed the bottle under a pile of stones in a conspicuous location along the shore. When Captain Metcalf opened the bottle, he found that another fur trader, an English ship's master out of Macao, had reached Kerguelen the preceding year.

The *Eleanora*'s sealing voyage to "Munsair Kurguland Land" was a failure; her crew discovered that "very few of the seals were furd ones." [13] The New York brig had departed from the island by the time the *Asia* of Nantucket and her sister ship *Alliance* reached Kerguelen late in December. Bound on a combined oil and sealing expedition, the crews of the New England vessels made their headquarters at a small harbor on the northern end of the island, which they named "Port Washington." They remained among the squalls and snows of Kerguelen for about ten weeks, during which time the master of the expedition died "amid great pain." [14] The seamen from the two Nantucket vessels mainly hunted the huge sea-elephant and carried their cargo of oil home to New England. In their spare time from the hunting ground, they gathered mussels from "Muss Bay" and shot wild fowl, particularly a species of teal which is found only on Kerguelen and its neighbors, the Crozets. After their departure in 1793, Kerguelen remained almost undisturbed by the China-trading sealing vessels for the rest of the period that ended with the War of 1812. Captain Mayhew Folger circled the island in 1807 searching for a harbor, but he made no attempt to land a gang of hunters. Instead, he took the *Topaz* on to New Zealand and the Pacific in the sealing voyage that discovered the *Bounty*'s colony on Pitcairn Island.

The other seal islands of the Indian Ocean—the Crozets, Marion, and Prince Edward—lie far to the west of Kerguelen and were also discovered by a French voyage of exploration in search of the great southern continent. Cook, who charted the islands four years later in 1776, named Marion Island in honor of the leader of the French expedition, Marion du Fresne, and the Crozets after his officer, Julien Crozet; Prince Edward Islands received an English designation. Prince Edward and Marion lie below the Cape of Good Hope and were known to American sealers and whalers who roamed the South Atlantic. The Crozets, however, were not discovered by the Yankee hunters for more than a decade after the initial New England vessel reached St. Paul. The pioneering ship at these remote and mountainous islands was the *Catherine* of New York, which set out in search of them in mid-1803, the year "the manuscript of the discoverer of Crozett Islands, was received." [15] The leader of the expedition, Captain Henry Fanning, first landed a sealing crew on Prince Edward Islands then worked the *Catherine* almost a thousand miles eastward before he located the Crozets. He touched at the southernmost isles, naming one "New York," another "Fanning," and the largest the "Grand Crozett." Making his anchorage at "Basin Harbor" on New York Island, he found the vessel amid a vast breeding ground of the southern fur seal.

Captain Fanning obtained a fine cargo of skins, left a sealing gang on New York Island, and returned to Prince Edward Islands. He had orders to leave a concealed report there of his discovery, if successful, for the master of the next ship the owners of the *Catherine* were sending out from New York to hunt the Crozets. As Prince Edward Islands were an established sealers' and whalers' rendzevous, the captain's instructions were designed to deceive the hunters there. Captain Fanning erected a pile of stones, conspicuously in the shape of a marking place, which satisfied the curiosity of the watchful sealers. Then, unobserved, he dug a hole at a designated distance from the marker, deposited a bottle containing his information and carefully replaced the earth. As soon as the *Catherine* was under sail, the men tore the marker apart and opened up the earth all around. But the bottle remained undisturbed until the sealing captain for whom it was deposited arrived and located it, much to the annoyance of the onlooking sealers.

The crew of the *Catherine* had not been able to peg and dry their fur skins at the bleak Crozets and carried their China cargo away from New York Island in a salted state. Sailing across the Indian Ocean toward the Java Sea, Captain Fanning brought the vessel to anchor at an uninhabited island near the Sunda Strait. The hunters landed their cargo in the small boats and began to peg and dry the skins on the deserted shore. However, shortly after landing, they noticed a Malayan proa enter and circle the bay and then beat off to the nearby coast of Sumatra. Captain Fanning guessed the outrigger was reconnoitering and that more pirate boats would follow after the initial appraisal of the size and strength of his ship. The New York sealing captain set the men to work constructing a redoubt on a small hill commanding the entrance to the bay. Their temporary fort was supplied with the ship's two six-pound guns and the crew divided into watches at the redoubt and on the vessel. A few days later, the sentry who was stationed in a tree gave the warning; a long line of outriggers was moving into the bay, unaware of the fort and the preparations on shipboard. Captain Fanning's sudden order to fire caught the pirates off guard, and after considerable damage to their boats, the Malayans fled to their retreat on the mainland.

Despite the precautions taken by Captain Fanning on Prince Edward Islands, the Nantucket sealing vessel *Favourite* found her way to the Crozets shortly after the *Catherine* reached Canton. Clearing from New England in the fall of 1804, she hunted at the islands for a few months early the following year. An English expedition that reached the Crozets after the War of 1812 found the hut built by the Nantucket sealers and many of their "tallies," pieces of wood on which the date "1805" was cut and the number of skins taken over designated periods of time.[16] The *Favourite* did not tarry long at the Crozets; like most of the sealing vessels of this period, she was attracted to the waters of the South Pacific. It was this area, whose center was the rich seal island of Más Afuera, that yielded the important cargoes of seal skins for the Canton market.

6

Más Afuera

The island of Más Afuera fulfilled, for a few crowded years, the seal hunters' dream of El Dorado. Located off the west coast of South America, where that legendary kingdom was also sought, the island was bright with the sealers' gold. Almost half a million of their prey were basking on the rocks when the first wave of American vessels reached Más Afuera, and many times more skins were carried from there to Canton than from all the other sealing areas combined. Only twice the size of St. Paul, the island supported, in its heyday, hundreds of seamen, with a dozen vessels lying off its dangerous shore. A number of the sealers did not belong to any ships; for many who settled on the island were solitary, independent hunters. They, and their fellow sealers in the organized gangs, lived in little huts, tended vegetable gardens, bartered among themselves, and traded with the visiting ships. They formed a strange colony thousands of miles from their Yankee homeland.

The colony on Más Afuera represented the overlapping activities of three waves of hunters who reached the island between

1798 and 1804. The seven-year period began with the rediscovery of the island by New England and New York sealing and whaling vessels and ended when the hunters were driven from their stronghold by the Spanish. The first American expedition to Más Afuera actually took place earlier, for a small New York vessel, the *Eliza,* acquired thirty-eight thousand skins there in 1792. When her master, William Stewart, brought the cargo to Macao the next year, he carried the first American shipment of seal skins to China direct from a hunting ground. But Captain Stewart's venture was a failure; he violated the trading regulations at Canton, was thrown into jail, paid a large fine, and sold his skins at the lowest price ever accepted by a contemporary American trader.

Half a dozen years passed before another Yankee sealing master followed Captain Stewart's trail to Más Afuera. Then, in 1798, the island was rediscovered for the sealers, and the first wave of hunters went ashore from seven vessels. Although no ships landed sealing gangs there in 1799, the attraction of Más Afuera was felt that year in the China-trader's ports from Long Island Sound to Massachusetts Bay. One of the mariners to carry home the legend was Amasa Delano, who had accompanied Captain Stewart on his unlucky trading venture at Canton. Sailing from Boston as the master of his own vessel, his was one of fourteen ships that reached the island in 1800. "The Lord have mercy on the sealers," exclaimed the supercargo of one of the last ships to arrive that year.[1] The third, and final, wave of hunters struck the island in 1803, when a dozen ships lay off the shore. "We arrived at the island of Massafuera the 8th. day of October, 1803," wrote the head of a sealing crew from Connecticut, "and were not a little surprised to find on the island more men than seals."[2] Two years later, the Spanish destroyed the settlement and cleared the island of all but one New England sealer.

Más Afuera is a small, volcanic island, about seven miles long and four miles wide. Situated five hundred miles off the coast of central Chile, it is one of the three islands of Juan Fernández. As the name suggests, Más Afuera ("more to sea") is the furthest of the group from land, about one hundred miles westward in the Pacific Ocean from the larger island of Más a Tierra ("more to land"). Más a Tierra was designated by the Yankee sealers simply as "Juan Fernández," and is usually referred to in their journals as the former abode of Alexander Selkirk, the prototype of Robinson Crusoe. At the time trade was inaugurated between the new United States and China, both Más a Tierra and Más Afuera were known as breeding grounds of the southern fur seal. An officer on the first American ship to reach Canton, which passed the islands in the spring of 1788, recorded more seals here than at any other place in the Atlantic or Pacific Oceans.[3] But when Más Afuera was rediscovered by the sealers a decade later, the neighboring "Juan Fernández" had been converted to a penal colony by the Spanish and was completely closed to the Yankee hunters.

The sealers refer to the "mountains" of Más Afuera; actually the island is a single mountain. The land, rising abruptly above the water, is broken into deep ravines, described as "romantic gulfs" by one of the early New England hunters, but more generally called "gulches."[4] Above the ravines, the island ascends in knolls to a high point of over six thousand feet; interspersed among the knolls were grassy slopes, the feeding grounds of wild goats. Because the "gulches" almost bisected the island at certain points, passage over or around the mountain—in pursuit of goats, to change sealing stations, or to visit—was long and difficult. The master of a New Haven gang makes the following entry for December 24, 1798: "I went round after breakfast to keep Christmas with Mr. Pease—got there at night."[5] The hunters prefered to traverse the island along the shore, although much of the land at sea level was obstructed by rocks and boulders that had crashed down from the heights above.

There was plenty of wood and water on Más Afuera at the end of the eighteenth century. A number of fresh-water streams ran through the ravines to the sea where casks were filled and transported in small boats to the vessels, or carried to the sealers' encampments that did not have their own source of water. Wood, too, was gathered from the ravines, where it was deposited during storms. The seamen also climbed the heights above the ravines and cut the timber from the slopes, tumbling the wood down to their comrades below. The abundance of wood and water, and the island's situation far enough at sea to escape the vigilance of the Spanish on the mainland, had long made Más Afuera a fueling station for English ships in the South Pacific. After the Revolution, the first American whaling vessels that rounded the Horn into the Pacific continued the English practice of visiting Más Afuera, and it was from them that the seal hunters at the Falklands learned of the rich harvest of skins to be gathered there.

The physiography of Más Afuera presented new problems to the vessels that arrived from sealing expeditions at the Falklands. There was very little level ground in the area where the men lived that was also convenient to the rocks where their prey was hunted. One of the few good areas was situated on the east side, near the watering station known as the "Landing"; another was the "Northwest Plains," on the west side. The Northwest Plains provided the largest level area for pegging skins, laying out vegetable gardens, and building huts. It was, however, two miles from a suitable landing, and there was no source of water, which had to be carried several miles from a pond on the opposite side of the island. And during the winter, in the southern hemisphere, pegging operations were retarded as the area lay in the shadow of the mountain for half of each day. Nevertheless, the Northwest Plains was the center of the island's activity in the seven years between its rediscovery as a sealing ground by Captain Edmund Fanning and the dispersal of the colony by the Spanish.

When Captain Fanning anchored the *Betsey* off the Northwest Plains early in 1798, he saw "3-400,000 seals presented to view." [6] And for the next ten weeks, the crew from the little New York brig slaughtered their prey among the rocks and boulders of Más Afuera until there was no more room for skins on the vessel. They stowed the hold first, then the cabin, and finally the forecastle, leaving barely enough room for the ship's company to sleep. With twenty thousand skins on board, the ninety-ton brig was ready to depart for Canton although her crew still had over four thousand pelts piled in stacks in caves on the shore. Seven men then volunteered to remain on the island and to add to the supply. Captain Fanning was sailing home direct from China, but he promised his New England sealers—the men had been recruited at New Haven and Stonington—he would arrange to have them picked up as soon as possible. In leaving a part of his crew behind to continue the hunt, Captain Fanning set the example followed by most of the shipmasters who reached the island over the next seven years. The captain usually designated the maximum time in which he or another vessel would return; after this period elapsed, the men were free to make any arrangements they could to get home to America.

A week after the *Betsey*'s sealing gang began what they thought was to be a life alone on the island, Captain Daniel Greene brought the *Neptune* abreast of the Northwest Plains. Both he and Captain Fanning had been at the Falklands when the news was spread by a Nantucket whaler of the great herds of fur seals on Más Afuera. Captain Greene hunted at the island about the same length of time as his predecessor when he, too, departed for China with a fine cargo, leaving behind his own gang of sealers. He also took on board Captain Fanning's men, who were anxious to get their additional skins to Canton and begin the homeward passage. Establishing his headquarters at the Landing, the head of the *Neptune*'s sealing gang noted a party of hunters from a New Bedford vessel encamped nearby on the Northwest Plains; their departure, four months later, he concluded: "left us here very lonesome."[7] But before the year ended, sealing crews from three other ships were living on the island and there was plenty of companionship.

In the first years of sealing at Más Afuera, when the gangs comprised six to a dozen men, and their prey existed in vast herds on the rocks, there was no hostility over "rights" to certain areas. The men hunted continuously and without restriction from one part of the island to another. And while each gang generally occupied a designated ground where they erected permanent huts and made their headquarters, they also put up temporary shelters and tents at the other places where they hunted. But when the fame of Más Afuera attracted an excessive number of hunters, and the sealing gangs became twice as large as the early ones, crews forcibly drove their competing comrades from designated areas. The head of a Nantucket gang, which held a part of the Northwest Plains early in 1803, described the defense of their territory: "Sent all hands round the cove to put a stop to Capt. Brintnall sealing." Several days later they "stopped Mr. Butler from destroying the clapmatches at the cove."[8] At the same time, two other Bay State vessels landed sealing crews on the Northwest Plains with the result, according to one of their supercargoes: "Capt. Wyer on shore to try to settle some treaty with Capt. Folger about killing."[9] Evidently the "treaty" was advantageous, for Captain Wyer arrived at Canton with almost sixty thousand skins.

The sealers improvised temporary accommodations on shore as soon as the site for their encampment was selected. They slept under rocks and ledges, with a tarpaulin or sail for additional protection; or, if a small boat could be spared, it was turned bottom up and used as a cover. In their improvised shelters, the men suffered from the rain, surf, ticks, and flys. Part of a day's entry in the journal of a member of an early sealing gang—"tormented with Buggs"—is preceded by similar complaints reflecting the seamen's discomfort in sleeping under the rocks while their permanent huts were being erected.[10] Provisions were stowed, like the seamen, under rocks, and covered with tarpaulin or seal skins. The usual stores were casks of bread and molasses, barrels of flour and salt provisions, and, sometimes, pipes of wine. When all their supplies were landed, the men who chose to remain on the island signed a contract with the captain, and, afterwards, celebrated with their shipmates. "The boats crew," wrote the master of a Connecticut gang that settled at the Landing, "brought a keg of whisky to drink farewell and stayed all night." [11] The vessel sailed the following day.

The hunters' first task, after their ship departed, was to erect permanent shelters at the sites selected for their headquarters. They constructed the frames for their houses from timber cut in the adjacent, wooded areas. The logs were either carried back to the headquarters or the frames were constructed in the woods and carted on the seamen's backs, sometimes for several miles, to the encampment. The houses varied in size; some were mere huts that held a single occupant, others were large enough for all or a part of the gang, requiring fifty rafters across the roof and almost a hundred large skins for covering. The sealers held "house warmings" when they moved into their huts; when they departed, they vacated them in the same spirit: "ship and crew landing at the log house which we give up with joy." [12] The wood-framed houses did not always prove snug enough for a second winter. The master of a New Haven crew recorded a part of the preparations for his second year on Más Afuera: "employed last night covering my stone house by moonlight." [13]

As soon as their huts were completed, the sealers took their places on the rocks, slaughtering an enormous number of seals in the period between the first wave of hunters in 1798 and the near depletion of the field in 1804. "I have carried more than one hundred thousand myself," wrote a Boston ship's master who estimated that three million seal skins were taken to Canton from Más Afuera in the seven-year interval.[14] One of the early gangs, a group of ten men encamped on the island in the summer of 1798, collected thirty-five thousand skins by the following spring, and sixty-four thousand more between then and the middle of November. Their leader expressed his men's sentiments at this moment: "gave three chears & qut sealing having got one hundred thousand." [15] But when their vessel came to pick them up several months later, they had another fifteen thousand to add to the quota. A seaman from the *Neptune,* one of a crew of twelve men who killed twenty-five hundred seals in a single day in mid-1799, suggests the spirit of the first years: "killing clapmatches from daylight till dark." [16] The slaughter could not continue forever. A crew of seven men from the *Minerva,* out of Newburyport, laboring on the island for almost six months late in 1803 and early 1804, obtained a cargo of only six thousand skins. Yet their haul was "nearly double any other gang of the same number." [17] They were one of the last American crews to hunt on the island.

Storing and "tending" such quantities of skins were often difficult and discouraging. The dried skins were packed in caves along the shore, insufficiently protected from the surf and the gales that beat against the island. A Connecticut seaman recorded the continual loss of the cargo in the caves, where the covers—"old wig skins"—blew off the stacks and their contents dispersed in the wind. "One stack," he noted, "of 2400 entirely blown away." [18] The leader of his sealing crew added: "lost about 300 skins last night by the surf." [19] The exposed, ironbound shore of Más Afuera, formed by rocks and boulders fallen from the mountain above, was often a dangerous place in which to work. The hunters complain of the falling rocks as a threat to both themselves and the prosecution of their trade, for the seals deserted the shore during the rock slides. The occasional earthquakes that shook the island were even more disruptive to sealing. Chile lies in the path of an earthquake belt running from Cape Horn to Alaska, and the effects of disturbances on the mainland were felt on Más Afuera, far out at sea. One "heavy" earthquake in 1799 kept the seals away for over a week while their hunters waited impatiently on the rocks.

The most serious disadvantage of the island's physiography was the total absence of harbors. The millions of skins taken at Más Afuera were loaded along the shore and carried through the surf in small boats to the vessel at great risks to both crew and cargo. An entry in a sealer's journal early in 1800—"get 17,000 off at 4PM when whale boat upset on the bar and 3 men drowned & 4 saved with great difficulty"—reveals the many dangerous trips between the shore and the vessel required to load the huge cargoes for China.[20] Transporting the skins from their stacks in the caves to the small boats was also difficult and dangerous, since the boats usually could not be beached adjacent to the stacking area. The sealers carried their loads, consisting of sixty to seventy skins, several miles over stones and boulders to the nearest landing.

There were only a few places around the island where vessels could anchor within one to two miles of the rocks. Sometimes, during the long loading operation, the ship lay as much as five miles off the shore. With most of the crew laboring on the rocks and in the small boats, the vessel was manned by a few hands and the supercargo. "I slept on shore one night only," wrote the supercargo of the *Neptune*, the second ship to load seal skins for China in 1798, "and I was full of blotches for a week."[21] Despite his reference to the ticks and flys that infested the island, the seamen record their own preference for duty ashore. Actually, the first two vessels that took part in the rediscovery of Más Afuera—the *Betsey* and the *Neptune*—were the only ones that lay on and off the island for as long as two months, a period that included the hunting as well as the loading of skins. The ships that followed put their sealing gangs ashore and then departed for periods ranging from several months to several years before returning to load the skins and pick up their men. In the interval, they made hunting excursions to the other seal islands of the South Pacific or they entered the ports along the mainland of Chile and Peru to carry on contraband trade, obtain provisions, or refit their vessels.

There were always some seamen on Más Afuera who did not have contracts with a ship's master or belong to a particular gang. Called "alone men" or "lopers," they received discharges or deserted at the island, or arrived there from the mainland after some misfortune, such as their vessel being confiscated by the Spanish. They sometimes outnumbered those hunting in organized crews. One of their spokesmen, William Moulton, estimated that in 1803 more than three-quarters of the two hundred men on the island did not belong to any ship. Moulton had been discharged from the *Onico* of Norwich after a continuous feud with the captain all the way from Connecticut. He was an example of the independent, conscientious Yankee who was always represented among the alone men at Más Afuera. "I resolved," he wrote, "to avoid insolent and ill-bred contradictions, and dogmatical abruptness from sailor officers, by a well timed civility, and by evading any particular intimacy." [22] He lived quietly in a hut on a cove, containing a table and cooking and sealing equipment purchased from another alone man for five hundred skins. After clearing the area around his house for a pegging ground, he worked diligently at his business, the occasional companion of equally sober New Englanders.

Representative of a less industrious type of alone man was the "Hermit Bill," who lived for many years in a cave on the island. He hunted just enough seals to obtain the bread and rum essential to his solitary existence. "He say he was never so happy before," noted a supercargo who traded him two gallons of rum for sixty fur skins, "there is no larboard watch, no reefing topsails, nobody to quarrel with, and he sleeps when he pleases and works when he pleases." [23] There were a number of easy-going seamen who chose to remain on Más Afuera because it offered equal opportunity for isolation or association. Originally, the men who remained alone were supplied with provisions and weapons from their ship, like the famous prototype of Robinson Crusoe who stayed alone on the neighboring island of Más a Tierra. But as the popularity of Más Afuera grew, the alone men were not so dependent upon their own resources. There was ample opportunity to trade with visiting ships, and they could rely on the goodwill of the more industrious hunters. The head of a sealing gang recorded sending six of his men "to help Lazy Walker get skins tho he deserves no help." [24] Walker had been discharged from a New Bedford whaler, the *Barclay*, one of the first American vessels to reach the island.

There was also a group of alone men, among whom the deserters figured prominently, who did little but gamble, drink, and steal. Sullivan Dorr called them "so many rascals," referring to the number who deserted there from his family's ships, having robbed them of provisions and skins. The most spectacular example of desertion occurred in 1803 when an entire ship's company abandoned the brig *Mentor*, leaving only her officers to man the vessel. The captain of another American ship, anchored in the vicinity of the near-empty brig, branded all the deserters living on the island "felons, pirates & murderers he that compleated the most hellish deeds is considered the cleaverist fellow & the most of a gentleman." [25] But not every mariner who wanted to desert was successful; the journals kept on Más Afuera record, too, the men that were "carried" back to their ships from hiding places on the mountain.

The alone men provided a significant source of skins for shipmasters bound for China. The usual arrangement, when skins were selling for approximately a dollar apiece at Canton, was to pay about sixty cents a skin on terms of one-third in cash, one-third on order, and one-third in provisions; if the price was entirely in currency, it was generally about fifty cents a skin. The charges for transporting the alone men's skins to China for sale, and for carrying the net proceeds in teas and silks back to America for them, was 15 to 25 per cent of the skins plus the customary freight rates; but charges were sometimes as high as one-third of the skins plus freighting expenses. Prices varied according to the sealer's needs, the most recent known sales at Canton, and whether the alone man was selling his skins outright for money and provisions, for sale at Canton to his account, or for a passage home. The ship's master generally tried to get one-half of the sealer's skins as the price for passage to America, either direct or via the trading port of Canton. If negotiations concerned a whole gang, with a considerable cargo of skins, a lower percentage was accepted. A crew of ten men, still on the island a year after the contract with their captain expired, and with over a hundred thousand skins, made an agreement to give up forty thousand for freight and passage to China and home.

Whether alone or members of a ship's crew, the sealers had plenty of opportunity to trade among themselves and with visiting vessels. They bartered a diversity of supplies: salt, garden seeds, twine, barley, duck cloth, peas, molasses, beef, tea, potatoes, coal, bread, sugar, pork, and clothing. The sealing and trading captains who touched at the island exacted a high price; a sealing gang in 1799 gave ten thousand skins for six pipes of bread, five barrels of flour, three barrels of salt provisions, and an old longboat the trader "was anxious to get rid of." [26] Tobacco and rum brought the highest prices. The head of a gang stationed at the Landing told how one of his hands "swam out for the keg of rum and nearly drowned bringing it in." [27] Nor were the seamen discouraged when an alone man warned that the captain who originally sold them good West Indian rum had substituted a New England variety, selling it at the same price.

An abundance of fish and water fowl were available to the hunters. "The best fishing I ever saw," noted the supercargo of the *Neptune* in 1798, observing that two men caught five hundred pounds of fish in a single hour.[28] The seamen fished in boats with hooks and lines or floated seal blubber on the water, using their clubs to kill the fish that were drawn to the bait. Cod and halibut were gathered from boats in great hauls, crawfish and lobsters were caught among the rocks and in the caves. There was plenty of wild fowl on the island, although the sailors' attempts to raise domestic fowl did not prove successful. They did, however, maintain flourishing vegetable gardens. "Our potatoes grow finely," wrote the master of a gang who maintained a garden at the Landing; he completed the story a few months later: "roasted potatoes for dinner—tasted better than anything I had since I left home."[29] The seamen cultivated peas, turnips, beets, parsley, cabbages, watermelons, and cucumbers as well as potatoes.

The wild goats of Más Afuera presented a brief threat to the vegetable gardens. Believed to be descended from the flock once tended by the original Robinson Crusoe on the neighboring island, they roamed the grassy slopes in large herds at the time the hunters rediscovered Más Afuera. "All hands agoating," noted a sealer in mid-1798, "caught 14."[30] At this time, the shipmasters described their crews killing twenty to thirty goats a day. The goats, whose meat was praised for its sweetness by the Yankee mariners, became so scarce by 1800 that several men, stalking the mountain for three or four days, often returned empty-handed. This prey, unlike most of the animal life on the island useful to the sealers, including the ten sheep originally grazing on the mountain, managed to survive their hunters by retreating to precipitous and inaccessible areas. The journals kept on the island recorded goat-hunting seamen stuck on ledges and in gullies from which it was most difficult to retrieve them.

During the winter season, when the top of the mountain was sometimes covered with snow, and it rained too hard to work along the shore or on the pegging ground, the sealers stayed in their huts. An unfailing indoor activity was making pegs out of old casks; a seaman could make five hundred in a day. They also carved plates out of wood, wrote letters home, studied seamanship from the books brought to the island, mended their clothes, or fashioned new ones. "Making a pair of trousers," wrote a seal hunter in July (winter in the southern hemisphere) of 1798, "set the waistbands on wrong and took them out again." His next entry: "Rainy day again. Finish trousers."[31] The men spent the late afternoons and evenings of rainy days visiting with each other, spinning yarns, and playing checkers. They recorded the gifts exchanged on these visits: a little tea, a pie of goat's meat, a handful of nuts, a few apples or oranges.

The sealers on Más Afuera observed the holidays they knew in their home towns in New York and New England. The head of a Connecticut gang told of his first Christmas on the island: "Dec. 25, 1798—Entertaining with stories and songs all day. Dec. 26—Keeping Christmas with seapie for dinner and some egg punch to wet the wissel."[32] One of his men described Christmas the following year: "Dec. 25, 1799—Last night had a dance. Seapie for dinner." His entry for the Fourth of July of that year suggests a less satisfactory holiday: "Stormy weather with nothing wetter Independence day with us."[33] Two years later, when over a hundred Americans gathered on the Northwest Plains to celebrate the Fourth of July, the Stars and Stripes waved from a high pole surrounded by thirteen mounds of rope yarn coiled around bundles of gunpowder. Representing the original colonies that gained independence, they were exploded in a loud and solemn ceremony.

One extraordinary holiday was New Year's 1801, when a New York vessel, the *Pegasus*, was chased to Más Afuera by two Spanish coastal patrol ships. She had been engaged in contraband trade on the mainland and had over forty thousand silver dollars on board. Anchoring off the Landing, her men managed to bury the money at the watering station just before their pursuers caught up with them. The Spanish confiscated the vessel, carrying away her crew as well as a number of sealers who were not quick or experienced enough to find hiding places. When the Spanish departed, the men came down from their mountain retreats, from which they had watched the *Pegasus*'s crew burying her treasure. They rushed to the pond, and "by wading, diving, raking, and every other means that could be put in requisition, every one got a large quantity of dollars."[34] After considerable fighting and stealing among themselves, some of the hunters formed gambling clubs, where—according to a disapproving alone man—"they have set thirty-six hours at a table without other cessation than to procure a little food and drink."[35] He identified one of the more tireless gamblers as an apostate Methodist minister who landed on the island as part of a New England sealing crew but made "drinking and carousing" his principal occupation.

Stealing was associated with more than buried treasure and gambling. One independent hunter, after transporting over a thousand skins across the island for sale in bundles of one hundred pelts each, was seized by the crew of the *Miantonomah* of Norwich and robbed of all his labor. Shipmasters who tolerated stealing and fighting among their crews were, sometimes, themselves directly guilty of theft and pillage. Discovering a quantity of unguarded skins drying on the ground, the captain of the *Hancock*, out of Boston, had them pulled from their pegs and transported to his ship even though they were marked with the hunter's initials. He also carried away a large copper kettle from the encampment and stove in the water casks. His depredation was observed, however, and news of it reached the vessel's agent at Canton who severely reprimanded the master. Some of the seamen even pilfered their own ship's supply of skins. "Detected our Blacks, five in number," wrote the captain of a Newburyport vessel in 1804, "taking skins from the cargo and selling them on shore and to ships."[36]

By this time, the American occupation of Más Afuera was drawing to a close. The commander of a Spanish patrol paid a friendly visit to the island in March 1804, informing the inhabitants of his orders to destroy the colony. He gave the sealing crews and the alone men four months to get their skins and provisions off the island. The few organized gangs still hunting among the rocks began an anxious vigil, their mood expressed by an earlier sealer on Más Afuera: "Many a look do I cast on the distant ocean to discry our ship & many a sigh for fear she will not come."[37] However, all but one of the vessels were trading or sealing in the coastal waters of Chile and Peru and they rescued their gangs before the deadline imposed by the Spanish.

They also took off the alone men willing to pay the high rates extorted for passage and freight to the offshore islands of Chile or to Canton and home. Their fee was a thousand skins for passage to the island of Santa Maria, below Valparaíso, a popular fueling station for Yankee vessels, which carried many of the sealers back to America.

Forty-six men were still living in their little huts on Más Afuera at the beginning of 1805, almost a year after the threat to destroy the colony. Half of them belonged to the *Huron,* the one New England sealing vessel with a gang on the island that was not in the vicinity of Chile or Peru when the Spanish imposed their deadline. She had acquired a cargo of twenty thousand hair-seal skins from the offshore islands of Santa Maria and Lobos, and returned to New Haven with her lading while a gang from the vessel remained on Más Afuera to kill fur seals. The other two dozen hunters were alone men, undecided as to when and how to quit the island. They, and a number of their comrades now gone, sold most of their skins to the supercargo of the *Huron,* who remained in charge of the gang on Más Afuera when the vessel returned to Connecticut. The supercargo had no money, but the alone men, wishing to be unencumbered by freight, accepted his note payable in America at thirty months from the date. In this manner, he acquired over ten thousand skins at an average of thirty-four cents apiece. Although not a great haul compared with the early years on Más Afuera, it exceeded the cargo taken by his own gang in over a year's work on the island.

The supercargo's skins were piled neatly in a cave below the Northwest Plains when the *Huron* returned to Más Afuera in mid-February 1805 to pick up her cargo for the Canton market. After the ship's lading was stowed, it was decided to make a final trip to the island of Santa Maria and land the last of the alone men to leave the threatened colony. Four members of the *Huron*'s gang remained behind to look after their supercargo's skins; there were also three independent hunters determined to stay on alone at Más Afuera. A few days after the vessel sailed, the Spanish brig arrived and its commander carried out his threat of a year's standing. The sealers were rounded up, their provisions, clothing, and houses destroyed, and their skins scattered in the wind, although the supercargo's stacks, once identified, remained unmolested.

One alone man was on the shore when the *Huron* anchored off the Northwest Plains three weeks after the destruction of the settlement. Escaping from the Spanish, he fled to a hiding place on the mountain, and now planned to remain as the single inhabitant of the island. He explained how the supercargo's skins had been spared and the four men left from the *Huron*'s gang and the two other independent hunters carried away as prisoners to the mainland. "We were sorry for their sakes, that our men were taken away," the supercargo wrote, "but it was really no damage to us, for we had really more men than we wanted." [38] However, their more benevolent Spanish captor put the men on vessels at Santa Maria and three of them actually reached home before their ship.

The lone survivor on the island, John Wright, with his two dogs, Rover and Bully, was visited by the crew from an American vessel in 1806. He told them he planned to remain for at least another five years, when he would have enough skins to return to his native Boston. There was no sign of him when Captain Barnard reached Más Afuera in 1815, on his long way home after a forced sojourn at the Falklands where the shipwrecked English seized his vessel. He found only the ruins of the seamen's huts and a few surviving plants from their vegetable gardens. There were no seals on the island.

7

The Southeastern Pacific

Más Afuera was the magnet that drew the American sealing vessels to the waters of the Southeastern Pacific. But the ships that anchored off the island's ironbound coast generally remained only long enough to land their sealing gangs. Then, with diminished crews, they headed for the mainland of Chile for provisions and contraband trade, or they sailed five hundred miles north from Más Afuera to the habitat of the fur seal on the islets of San Félix and San Ambrosio or an equal distance southeast to trap the hair seal or refit their vessel on the islands of Mocha and Santa Maria. The latter island, whose green hills were then covered with wild roses, was the most popular rendezvous for Yankee vessels in the southern hemisphere. But the sealers' cruising ground in the Southeastern Pacific was much wider than a thousand-mile arc radiating from Más Afuera. The hunters sought their prey further north, along the coast of Peru, and, from there, westward to the Galápagos Islands. They pursued the seal southward almost to the Strait of Magellan, and hunting far out across the Pacific, they reached Sala-y-Gomez, Easter, and Pitcairn islands.

At least half of the Yankee ships hunting the offshore islands of Chile and Peru did not have Canton as their destination, although they usually had a crew on Más Afuera slaughtering the fur seal. They sought the hair seal and the illicit trade of the Spanish colonial ports. These sealing expeditions returned home with their cargoes of fur and hair skins, or combined sealing and whaling voyages, their ladings of skins and oil destined for American or European markets. In a few exceptional cases, sealing vessels actually made two passages: after returning to New England with hair skins, they retraced their track to Más Afuera, where they loaded fur skins for Canton. The China-bound sealing vessels, with gangs on Más Afuera, also cruised along the coasts of Chile and Peru, seeking an opportunity to enter the mainland ports for their share in the contraband trade. And while they rarely hunted the hair seal on the offshore islands, they sought the fur seal on the more remote rocks of San Félix and San Ambrosio, far out at sea from the mainland.

In 1792, the year the initial American sealing expedition reached Más Afuera, Captain Josiah Roberts anchored the *Jefferson* off the islets of San Félix and San Ambrosio, five hundred miles off the northern coast of Chile. "I am fully convinced," wrote his first officer, "that there is not a more barren spot on the face of the earth." [1] The two small islands, separated by a dozen miles of reefs, were considered by Captain Roberts as a single area, which he designated "St. Ambrose." However, he said the most westward of the two was shaped like a shoe and so named by his crew. "Shoe Island" is actually San Félix, a barren area a mile and a half long, yet slightly larger than the neighboring San Ambrosio. The fur trader James Colnett, visiting the islets a year later, described them as barren rocks in whose "craggy breaks and shelvings, seals have found a resting place." [2] He noted the decayed carcasses littering the narrow beaches, but did not know it was a Boston China-trader, Captain Roberts, who had preceded him to the desolate spot.

When Captain Roberts reached the islands, mid-way on his

passage to the Northwest Coast, the rocks were covered with seals. He immediately sent off a boat with his officers and a dozen hands to begin the slaughter, but they were unable to make a landing for five days. The coast of both islets is stony and precipitous, without good anchorage for a ship, and only a few places to beach a small boat. The men finally found a narrow track of sand on the west side of San Félix, relying on rope ladders to scale the steep walls of rock. During the ten weeks the crew hunted the two islands, they slept on shipboard. There was no water on San Félix and only a limited supply on San Ambrosio, although the islets were plagued with flies. "As sure as you open your mouth," cautioned the master of the *Minerva* out of Newburyport, "you will catch it full of flies at the time when I was striving to keep my mouth & nose clear of them so as to breath I hapned to take off my hat to my perplexity when put it on again I had at least one pint of flies in the crown of it." [3] Feeding on the flies, and the fish, were hordes of waterfowl which the sealers hunted in their spare time.

After the rediscovery of Más Afuera by the Yankee sealers six years later, a number of the shipmasters with gangs there followed Captain Robert's lead to San Ambrosio and the more popular San Félix. The second wave of hunters pitched tents or erected shelters on the beaches or brought the frames for their huts with them from Más Afuera. When there was more than one gang on the tiny islets, competition between the sealers was intense. A crew of seven men from the *Concord* of Salem remained on San Félix for over a month in the first year of the nineteenth century and obtained only seventeen hundred skins. Their rivals were a gang of six seamen from the Boston ship *Alexander,* whose leader supplied the North Shore crew with liberal portions of rum. When the Salem supercargo saw that his men, as a result, were unable to work, he sent them on shipboard for floggings "which is very disagreeable but there is no help for it." [4] The Boston rivals, unknown to them at the time, were in an extremely precarious situation; their captain, after leaving them on the islets, lingered at Hawaii in "a licentuous manner," never returned for his men on San Félix, and eventually committed suicide by jumping from his ship.[5] The abandoned hunters were finally rescued by a New Haven sealing captain who got one-half of their twelve thousand skins in return for their passage to Canton and home.

The first American sealing crew on San Ambrosio and San Félix was warmly received at Valparaíso when they entered the coastal waters of Chile in mid-1792 after stopping at Más a Tierra. Although the neighboring island to Más Afuera was now a penal colony, the commandant allowed the hunters from the *Jefferson* to come ashore and supplied them with provisions. He gave Captain Roberts a letter to the commandant at Valparaíso, where the vessel visited before commencing her sealing expedition at San Félix and San Ambrosio. The commandant at Valparaíso was particularly interested in the Boston vessel's charts and books, which he sent to Ambrose Higgins, the governor at the capital city of Santiago. "Don Ambrosio O'Higgins" wrote the sealing captain a letter, returning his books and charts, and the ship's sea-paper bearing the signature of President Washington "whose imortal name I have had infinite satisfaction to see stamped for the first time by his own hand . . . . a hand & arm so dextrously strong & fatal to the British Empire & no less beneficient to the happy country that gave him birth."[6] Supplied with thirty bushels of potatoes, two bullocks, eight hogs, ten dozen fowl, two thousand onions, and an assortment of pumpkins, cabbages, lemons, oranges, and nuts, the *Jefferson* left Valparaíso for the hunting ground five hundred miles to the north.

A decade later, when the American colony at Más Afuera was well established and a number of vessels ploughed the water between the island and the mainland, the Yankees were not so well received. Officially, no foreign vessel could put into a Spanish colonial port except under extreme necessity, in circumstances when it would be inhuman to deny the vessel a haven, equipment, or provisions. The plea of distress was generally advanced by any ship's master with articles to trade, and the success of the plea depended upon the vigilance of the commandant, who was, in turn, influenced by local or international conditions. Chile was one of the most remote of the Spanish colonies in South America, and the attraction of the Yankee trading articles, especially wearing apparel, linen, cotton, and woolen goods, and the "notions" for which the New Englanders were becoming famous, was difficult for the local administrators to resist. A strict adherence to law was less usual in the secondary ports, where a show of force by the intruding vessel was also more respected. On the other hand, the smaller ports had fewer provisions and Spanish dollars, the silver specie prized by American captains and supercargoes trading at Canton.

It was generally impossible for an American ship's master to determine, in advance, his reception at the ports of Chile and Peru. Once inside the harbor, his vessel might be allowed to trade, refit, and provision; be ordered out immediately; or be confiscated. In the first years of the nineteenth century, the United States was not always considered "the happy country" designated by Don Ambrosio O'Higgins a decade earlier. Spain had assisted the American colonies in their war for independence, and the Chilean governor's admiration for Washington expressed both Spanish and Irish hatred for an old enemy. After the execution of Louis XVI and the victories of France's revolutionary armies in Italy, the rulers of Spain sensed the possible consequence in South America of their earlier support of the American Revolution. The Americans, barely established as the United States, were already well known, wherever they went, as the advocates of independence. Visiting Valparaíso in 1802, a New England China trader distributed Spanish translations of the Declaration of Independence "For the better promotion of the embryo cause." [7] With revolution and counter-revolution sweeping Europe, Spain's bureaucrats in the new world reflected

Captain Daniel Greene
of the *Neptune*.
From the collection of
the New Haven Colony
Historical Society.

William Mariner,
a beachcomber of Tonga.
From Mariner, *An Account
of the Natives of the
Tonga Islands* (London, 1817).

The *Betsey* of New York, Captain Edmund Fanning.
From Fanning, *Voyages Round the World* (New York, 1833).

Captain Barnard's house at the Falklands.
From Barnard, *A Narrative of the Sufferings and Adventures of Capt. Charles H. Barnard* (New York, 1829).

Hunting seals off the coast of Peru.
From Barnard, *A Narrative of the Sufferings and Adventures of Capt. Charles H. Barnard* (New York, 1829).

Seals on the Island of St. Paul. From Captain Péron's drawing, *Memoires du Capitaine Péron, Sur Ses Voyages* (Paris, 1824).

The Island of St. Paul.
From Pinkerton, *Voyages and Travels* (London, 1812).

The Island of Más Afuera.
From Anson, *A Voyage Round the World* (London, 1748).

Sealers' encampment in the South Seas.
From Fanning, *Voyages Round the World* (New York, 1833).

The massacre at Wailea Bay on Sandalwood Islands. From Dillon, *Narrative and Successful Results of a Voyage to the South Seas* (London, 1829).

Hunters from the *Dromo* at the Island of Cedros.
From Little, *Life on the Ocean; or Twenty Years at Sea* (Boston, 1845).

King Tamaahmaah visiting the *Dromo* at Hawaii.
From Little, *Life on the Ocean; or Twenty Years at Sea* (Boston, 1845).

Captain Porter's drawing of the American anchorage at Nuku Hiva. From Porter, *Journal of a Cruise Made to the Pacific Ocean* (New York, 1822).

The anchorage at Whampoa, *c.* 1800. Courtesy of the Peabody Museum of Salem.

The foreign factories at Canton, *c.* 1800. Courtesy of the Peabody Museum of Salem.

China Street, Canton. From Wathen, *Journal of a Voyage to Madras and China* (London, 1814).

the difficulties of the home government at Madrid which represented the monarchal houses of Bourbon and Parma and at the same time was an ally of France in her wars with England.

When the Yankees began their colony on Más Afuera, and appeared in increasing numbers in the coastal waters of Chile and Peru, their nation was less than twenty years old. In some of the remote parts of the Spanish empire, the citizens of the United States were considered by local authorities as English, and, consequently, treated as enemies. A Boston sealing captain who visited the coast many times over a five-year period at the turn of the century claimed to have secured freedom from the prison at Lima for over fifty seamen whom "the Spanish considered as Englishmen, which included pretty much all foreigners."[8] However, most crews of American ships in the South Pacific at this time did include a number of English, Irish, and Scottish nationals. Furthermore, it was the practice of American sealing and trading vessels along the west coast of South America to carry two flags and two sets of papers, their own and an English forgery, in order to benefit, if possible or necessary, from the protection and advantages of British maritime and commercial power. A Yankee ship's master, with little or no information about the political situation in Europe, was never certain, when he hoisted the English union or showed his forged papers, whether a state of war existed between the governments at Madrid and London. English privateers operating in the same area often followed the Yankee custom, and carried the Stars and Stripes as well as the Union Jack. One privateer, prominently displaying the American colors, plundered and burned villages up and down the coast of Chile for over a year.

The Yankee sealing captains usually attempted to enter the coastal ports of Chile and Peru whether their reception was friendly or hostile. An alone man on Más Afuera condemned the "iniquitous practice" whereby the ship's company, not hired for the business of smuggling, is exposed to the possibility of long terms in jail.[9] But the crews were generally as eager as their captains to visit the towns of Valparaíso, Concepción, Lima, and Coquimbo. The trading articles their vessels carried were purchased at high prices, in silver, by the local merchants, which promised a richer cargo at Canton from which all members of the venture might profit; while the need or desire for provisions as well as the hope for diversions on shore also united the ship's company in their attempt to force, if necessary, their way into the coastal harbors. Wine was available cheap in taverns for immediate consumption or in casks for the vessel; bullocks, sheep, pigs, and domestic fowl were purchased in great quantities, along with potatoes, cabbages, squashes, and pumpkins. There was, too, a fine variety of fruits—apples, peaches, pears, plums, cherries, and melons—that held great appeal to seamen who had lived for months on victuals from ship's store or seal island.

If the American vessel was ordered out, and the captain refused to depart voluntarily, the Spanish generally made a show of force or cut the cables and towed the ship to sea. The master of a Newburyport sealing vessel acknowledged two failures, in 1803, to anchor in the harbor at Valparaíso: "Whilst we like the wandering Jews in a state of exile find the boistrous main our mildest retreat and only asylum." [10] He was not so docile, however, at the smaller and less strongly fortified port of Coquimbo, where he prepared the vessel for a fight when ordered out. In his case, the Spanish commandant capitulated to the Yankee resistance and gave the ship a two weeks' haven to make repairs and trade with the merchants of the port and the surrounding towns. When American vessels were allowed anchorage at the more important harbors of Lima and Valparaíso, a watch was often kept on the crew, who were not allowed on shore without an officer, and were restricted in their movements and forced to return to the ship to eat and sleep. "We are kept so close here," wrote the supercargo of a Connecticut vessel at Valparaíso in 1801, "that I had rather be to sea where there is no limitation." [11] But the limitations were not always so severe in practice. The journals of the sealers also contain references to sightseeing, public celebrations, and visits to taverns and private houses in the major cities of Chile and Peru.

A few sealing vessels were seized by the Spanish in the ports of Valparaíso and Lima, generally at the time most of their crews were hunting on Más Afuera. The usual charge was giving information and supplies to the English privateers that lurked along the thousands of miles of coast between the Galápagos Islands and the Strait of Magellan. Generally, the vessels were restored after a period of time, during which the ship's master and crew were confined to a limited area of the town, or, in a few extreme cases, kept in jail. One of the most serious incidents involved the confiscation of a Norwich vessel at Valparaíso in 1802 with a cargo of sixty thousand seal skins.[12] After a long confinement on land, during which the skins were ruined, the Chilean government reimbursed the captain for his losses and allowed the ship's company to take berths on other sealing and whaling vessels in the area. A sister ship from Norwich was seized at the same time, but most of her skins and crew were on Más Afuera, where her seamen joined the ranks of the alone men.[13] Her captain eventually sold the vessel to the Spanish, remaining at Valparaíso under mysterious circumstances. After turning over the money from the sale of his vessel to a resident of the town, he became seriously ill and was hidden from his fellow New England sea captains, who visited the house frequently over the next three years without knowing that the Connecticut ship's master was concealed there. When Amasa Delano discovered his friend in the house in 1805, in a state of starvation, he brought him a kettle of soup each day from his own ship. Despite Captain Delano's efforts to remove the sick mariner, the Norwich master died shortly after making a will in favor of his landlord.

Captain Amasa Delano was a familiar figure in the principal ports of Peru and Chile during the half-dozen years he and his brothers sought the fur seal throughout the South Pacific. His most famous encounter with the Spanish developed from what he calls the "Tryal affair." After leaving a sealing gang on San Félix and San Ambrosio in the first month of 1801, Captain Delano took his vessel southward to the Yankee seamen's rendezvous at the island of Santa Maria. Early one morning in February, he saw a Spanish ship enter the harbor, and as she did not show her colors, he sent a boat alongside, noting that the decks were lined with slaves. The captain of the vessel, Beneto Cereno, told Captain Delano that his ship, the *Tryal,* was completely without water. The Boston sealer then sent water to the *Tryal,* but as he departed in the boat for his own ship, he was astonished to see Captain Beneto Cereno leap from the deck into the boat, with a cry that caused other Spanish sailors to jump overboard or fly up the rigging, as high as they could go, calling out for help. Captain Cereno said the slaves had captures his ship and killed many of the Spanish crew, and he appealed to the New England mariner to retake the vessel. The slaves cut the *Tryal's* cables and were drifting to sea when Captain Delano got two boats of armed men alongside and finally boarded her, after an ugly battle in which five of his men were wounded. When the Boston captain arrived on deck, amid a scene he described as "truly horrid," he could barely control the Spaniards' desire for revenge. The *Tryal* was taken to Concepción where Captain Delano entered a claim of eight thousand dollars for services against Captain Cereno who owned the ship and part of her cargo, which originally included seventy-two Senegalese slaves destined for Lima. Captain Cereno did everything possible to avoid payment, but the viceroy supported Delano's claims. When he finally got his money, the Boston sealing captain picked up his gang on San Félix and headed for the Galápagos Islands.

"American citizens and seamen," noted a Connecticut sealer concerning the coast of Chile in 1803, "are dispersed throughout this part of the globe."[14] Many were deserters from vessels hunting the hair seal and refitting at Mocha and Santa Maria, the latter island the scene of the battle for the *Tryal.* "In the course of the night," according to the supercargo of a Salem vessel at Santa Maria in 1800, "two of our sealers stole the yawl and ran on shore with all their clothes." A week later, he added: "Moser, one of our hands gave us the slip . . . we saw him on the beach, sent the boat after him, but he ran in the woods." [15] Another New England sealing vessel, hunting between Santa Maria, Más Afuera, and Australia, lost seventeen of its original crew through desertion. The deserters' flight to the mainland was not always a direct route to the taverns and waterfront areas of Concepción, where the ladies "are rather partial to the Americans and to Englishmen." [16] A British fur trader at Santa Maria in 1800 described how the Indians of the neighboring mainland towns, on horseback, captured American seamen by "casting a rope with a slip knot on the end, forming a noose, and immediately driving away with speed." [17] If the deserting sailors escaped the lasso, they were frequently robbed by the natives of the villages through which they passed on their way to the larger towns.

The authorities and the citizens of the major ports appear to have been fairly tolerant of the Yankee seamen, considering the magnitude of the American's activities on Santa Maria and Mocha, which are a part of the mainland of Chile and not, like Más Afuera, five hundred miles at sea. Santa Maria forms the southwestern tip of the crescent-shaped bay which includes the harbor of Concepción on the north. The more southern island of Mocha is situated about fifteen miles from the mainland. Both islands originally belonged to a family called Santa Maria who occupied the island bearing their name until Spain and England commenced a long period of intermittent warfare in 1780. The islands were then evacuated by the settlers from the mainland and became a haven for British privateers and American sealing and whaling vessels. Santa Maria had good anchorage, wood, and water, and an abundance of provisions. The orchards planted by the initial settlers continued to bear apples and peaches for the interlopers of Old and New England, and the deserted gardens yielded peas, potatoes, cabbages, strawberries, and blueberries.

After the original families and their dependents abandoned the island, Santa Maria was overrun with wild hogs, which the mariners hunted to extinction. They also hunted the wild fowl and their eggs, especially those of the gull, which the seamen prized for their sweet taste.

Most Yankee sealing vessels visited Santa Maria while their main crews were hunting on Más Afuera. They came to refit and provision; they also transported alone men from Más Afuera who settled on Santa Maria while waiting for berths on sealing and whaling ships bound home to New England and New York. At various times during the heyday of sealing in the South Pacific, between 1798 and 1804, there were a dozen American vessels anchored at Santa Maria, their crews ashore shooting, fishing, playing ball, and "exchanging civilities." The alone men, while waiting for berths, built themselves huts and worked with the gangs hunting the hair seal along the island's twelve-mile perimeter. They found the competition there as intense as on Más Afuera, with shipmasters or gang leaders defending their rights to certain hunting areas, and distributing rum and misinformation to every newcomer.

The island of Mocha, approximately the same size as Santa Maria, lies eighty miles to the south. With a safe harbor and plenty of wood and water, it was the second most-visited of the hair seal islands along the west coast of South America. However, Mocha and Santa Maria yielded only a limited number of skins compared with the great hauls of fur skins taken at Más Afuera. One of the most successful expeditions, hunting the two islands for three months in 1798, acquired about fourteen thousand hair skins.[18] This expedition, which reached the islands from New York, put ashore at Mocha nine men who lived for almost two weeks under a leaky boat in cold and rainy weather before completing a hut for themselves and a fenced yard to corral the hair seals. On their first trial, they drove four thousand seals from the rocks toward the "seal yard"; about one thousand died in the heat of the day, fifteen hundred were herded into the yard by dusk, and the other fifteen hundred were kept between the rocks and the yard during the night and driven in at dawn. The congestion within the yard was so great that the seals broke the fences and all but eight hundred escaped. The yard was rebuilt and by continuously repeating the process, the gang on Mocha salted eight thousand hair skins during the time their shipmates on Santa Maria obtained about six thousand.

The relatively large cargo of hair skins taken at Mocha was duplicated five years later when a small gang from a Connecticut vessel hunted for four months on the island of Santa Maria.[19] The success of their expedition was assured when the supercargo defied the captain and remained on Santa Maria with six men while the vessel sailed for the offshore islands of Peru. Although it appeared to the captain that there were no seals on Santa Maria, the supercargo noted that, beyond the beach strewn with the blood and carcasses of previous slaughter, a few hair seals kept coming into the shallow water and looking toward the beach. Deciding that the seals wanted to come there, but were frightened by the terrifying condition of the beach, he set his small gang to cleaning up the sandy area adjacent to the water. The men carried all the carcasses down to the sea, to drift out with the tide, and washed and raked the sand stained with blood. Then the seals began to return, at first only a few at a time, but finally enough to keep the hunters busy all day. By the time their own slaughter had returned the beach to its former state, the men had obtained eight thousand skins.

The island of Lobos de Tierra in Peru was the principal destination for the vessels that hunted along the mainland—several thousand miles north from Mocha and Santa Maria. On the way to Lobos from the latter islands, the Yankee sealers searched most of the offshore islets and rocks, especially the tiny Bird Islands about twenty miles from the coast northwest of Coquimbo. These two islands, which contained no water and only a few places to beach a boat, were generally included in the hunters' expedition since they were the habitat of both the fur and the hair seal. The islets yielded a limited harvest of skins to the small gangs who remained on the rocks and ledges while their vessels were obtaining salt and provisions at Coquimbo.

The commandant at Coquimbo was more hospitable to the Americans than was his fellow administrator at Valparaíso, making his port popular with sealing and trading vessels and, consequently, a center for deserters. Captain Amasa Delano, whose South Pacific sealing voyages were particularly plagued by deserters, nevertheless wrote lyrically of the great bay of Coquimbo, whose "lofty Andes in the interior rise mountain over mountain as far as the eye can reach, with awful sublimity." [20] The merchants at Coquimbo, like those of many of the smaller ports of Chile and Peru, generally traded with the Yankees whether they were officially welcomed or not—the American visitors making their arrangements and completing their transactions as discreetly and as quickly as possible. A Boston sealing and trading vessel, visiting one of the secondary ports of Chile at the beginning of the nineteenth century, brought the local merchants on board in the late afternoon and completed all sales by midnight, when the purchases were stowed in the small boats and sent ashore. When trade was more open and leisurely, the crew members and local residents formed friendly relations, and the descendants of New England Puritans were presented with rosaries and crucifixes to protect them on the voyage ahead.

The island of Lobos de Tierra attracted most of the American vessels that hunted along the coast of Chile and Peru. The hunters at Lobos were generally provisioned from Pisco, where the authorities were more friendly than those at the capital, Lima. The sealers used Lobos as a salting station for the hair skins acquired there as well as from other areas, including the more seaward Lobos Afuera. For Lobos was convenient to the salt marshes of Sechura, a desert area further north near the border of Ecuador. The master of the *Dispatch,* out of Newburyport, whose crew spent almost a week gathering salt near Sechura Bay, recorded that when his men returned to the ship "all coats have a coating of salt." [21] When his vessel reached Lobos, a part of the crew processed five thousand hair skins in the two-week period their shipmates hunted the hair seal along the island's fifteen miles of rocky shore. Lobos was the last important stop on the west coast of South America for the sealing vessels which then headed across the Pacific to the Galápagos Islands.

The six-hundred-mile sail from Lobos to the Galápagos, which lie directly along the equator, was never rewarded by a rich haul of skins. Although one of the most tireless New England hunters in the South Pacific suggested a vessel might obtain several thousand skins there, and the seamen's journals kept at Galápagos often refer to seals in the vicinity of the islands, the only really extensive sealing activity was when a vessel occasionally overhauled a lading of skins there on the way to China. It was the giant tortoise that comprised the extraordinary cargo the Yankee mariners hunted at the Galápagos. These ancient reptiles gave the islands their original and popular name—*galápago* is the Spanish word for giant tortoise—although they now officially bear the designation of Archipelago de Colón. When the American sealers reached the islands they bore English names bestowed upon them in the seventeenth century by the buccaneers who used the Galápagos as a base from which to attack Spanish ships and the mainland towns of South America. The Spanish had discovered the islands early in the sixteenth century, and these first European visitors ashore expressed astonishment at the giant reptiles and the tameness of the birds and disappointment over the lack of fresh water. During the next two and a half centuries conditions on the islands, never inhabited by the Spanish, remained relatively unchanged. And when the American sealers landed at the Galápagos, they, too, marveled at the reptiles and the birds and searched, often in vain, for fresh water.

Called "The Enchanted Islands" by the early Spanish visitors, the Galápagos nevertheless presented an uninviting shore to the sealing vessels seeking anchorage among the thirteen islands that comprise the archipelago. The bays of the main islands were lined with mangroves that soon thinned out before an almost impenetrable thicket of shrubs and bushes. Hacking their way through the underbrush, the sailors entered a rocky and parched region, the habitat of the prickly pear cactus that provided food for the giant tortoises and the land iguanas. But above this arid region, about a thousand feet up the slopes of the volcanic craters that comprise the islands, they discovered an enchanted area, a region of lush vegetation, watered by rain clouds that hang over the mountain craters for at least half of each year. High up in the clouds—the largest island has an elevation of over five thousand feet—were the open craters whose rims and interior walls were lined with scarred and ragged lava that burned and blistered the sealers' feet.

"Leave this port this Day With 250 Turpen 8 Boat Load Wood" reads a sentence from a letter deposited in 1812 by a New England vessel at the sailors' post office on Charles Island, the most popular rendezvous for American ships at the Galápagos.[22] The giant tortoise, usually called terrapin by the Yankee visitors, was gathered in great hauls and placed alive on shipboard, where it lived for a number of months without food or water. The sailors prized them not only as fresh meat, but as a defense against scurvy. The *Dromo* of Boston, sailing from the Galápagos in 1808 to participate in the pioneering seal hunt off the coast of Lower California, carried away a supply of turtles that lasted three months, during which time the mess was served "turtle soup as common as pea soup; and terrapin pies as much so as salt beef." [23] Another Boston sealing ship carried three hundred terrapin to Más Afuera, although more than half of them died after being landed on the island and eating grass. The supercargo of a New York vessel hunting in vain for seals at the Falklands in 1805 was presented with a "lean" terrapin by the master of a ship bound home from Más Afuera. "It appears rather a cruel assertion, when acted upon," he wrote, "that these animals live four to six months without any food." [24] An English sailor, who left the Galápagos Islands in 1814, claims he carried a giant tortoise all the way home, where it lived for ten months before being killed "by an act of kindness." When the tortoise had appeared drowsy, the sailor's wife, thinking that it was cold, placed it before the fire; she returned several hours later to find only a pool of melted fat beneath the shell.[25]

The American seamen generally preferred the giant tortoise and the sea or "green" turtle for their live cargo, although Captain David Porter of the *Essex* referred to the "timid guanas" which his men took by the hundreds to their ship.[26] Captain Porter, who visited the islands during the War of 1812, said his men found the iguana an excellent meat, many preferring it to the turtle. Both the giant tortoise and the land iguana roamed the bleak, arid lower regions of the larger islands, feeding on the buds of the prickly-pear cactus which provided food for the hunters as well as for the hunted. The seamen cut the pears from the cactus with long poles to which they fastened sealing hooks, with four men holding a sheet at each corner to receive the falling fruit. The pears, strung in netting between the cabin beams, kept fresh for several months. The tame birds of the island also proved an easy prey to the hunters, particularly the dove and the young booby. Three or four sealers often killed six dozen doves in a few hours. However, one seaman, who described the boobies "as delicacy as squab," also told how a shipmate, climbing a tree to catch boobies, fell to his death on the rocks below.[27]

The mangroves that grew along the water's edge provided a good supply of wood, but fresh water was not so readily available. The three islands most visited by the Yankee sealers—Albemarle, James, and Charles—generally provided some supply of water, although it often required a long search to locate the source. Captain Porter found a cask of water "bountifully" left near the post office on Charles Island for distressed seamen who might not have knowledge or strength to find the spring of water in the center of the island. The post office, located at a popular harbor on the northwestern tip of the island, was a box nailed to a post bearing a sign which read "Hathaway's Postoffice." It was the custom for mariners to deposit their letters there, in bottles, which the first ship bound home would carry away. Captain Porter, who commanded a frigate in the South Pacific during the War of 1812, used the information contained in letters at Hathaway's Postoffice to acquaint himself with the maneuvers of British privateers, whalers, and trading ships in the area. He also purposely left a great deal of misinformation at the post office concerning his own maneuvers, as well as depositing misleading information in bottles on the neighboring James Islands. An English visitor to James Island in 1814 described the grave of an American ship's officer who was killed in a duel there with a fellow seaman.

On the opposite side of Charles Island from Hathaway's Postoffice, there existed a strange little settlement called Pat's Landing, named after Patrick Walkins, an English seaman who lived there in the early years of the nineteenth century. He built a hut about a mile from the shore and somehow managed to cultivate a few surrounding acres in potatoes and pumpkins which he traded to the visiting ships for rum or money. He was described as dressed in rags, covered with vermin, and having a great, matted beard of red hair. Although his ambition seemed merely to get a sufficient supply of rum, on one occasion he tried to capture a Negro sailor who came to the landing from a Nantucket vessel. The American seaman subdued the assailant and carried him to the ship, which lay in the harbor alongside an English smuggler. Patrick Walkins was severely whipped aboard both vessels and forced to disclose the hiding place of his money, which the combined crews robbed of five hundred dollars and then destroyed his hut and garden. During the next few years, Patrick successfully repeated his attempt to capture visiting seamen, with a liberal use of rum, and finally had five sailors dependent upon him, working as his slaves. All six men departed in 1809 in an open boat, allegedly for the Marquesas; but only Patrick Walkins was in the boat when it arrived at the port of Guayaquil on the coast of Ecuador. The lone survivor searched there for a native wife, but was confined to the local prison before he had a chance to return with her to his island domain.

The Galápagos were generally the outermost limit for the sealing expeditions from Más Afuera and the offshore islands of Chile and Peru. After taking on their cargoes of "terrapin," the Yankee ships headed back to the west coast of South America or on to their trading destination at Canton. But a few adventurous shipmasters, like Captains Amasa and Samuel Delano, searched Sala-y-Gomez and Easter Island, and another New Englander, Captain Mayhew Folger, found the *Bounty's* colony on Pitcairn Island while in quest of the seal away off in the middle of the great South Pacific. Captain Folger brought the Boston vessel *Topaz* off Pitcairn Island early in 1808. He recorded his surprise to see smoke rising from the island, as "Cartwritt," the history of whose voyage Captain Folger had on board, described the island as uninhabited.[28] But the captain was even more surprised when a boat paddled out from the shore and its three occupants hailed him in the English language, presenting a gift of coconuts. They brought Captain Folger ashore to meet the patriarch of their island, an old mariner named Alexander Smith, who told the New England sea captain the hitherto unknown story of the fate of the *Bounty*.

Alexander Smith described himself as the last of the English seamen who landed on Pitcairn Island almost two decades earlier, and revealed the saga of violence and bloodshed that followed in the wake of the mutiny on the *Bounty*. He told how the mutineers set their captain and eighteen loyal officers and men adrift in the ship's launch on an April morning in 1789, and then sailed back to Tahiti. Sixteen of the men elected to remain there while Fletcher Christian and eight of their shipmates set out for the more southern island of Tubuai. After a period of violence on the latter island, Christian and six of the mutineers, along with twelve women, an infant girl, and six native men, reached Pitcairn Island in January 1790, and established their hidden refuge on its ironbound shore. Running the *Bounty* aground, and burning her, they set up a colony which was allowed only a few years of peace before a series of destructive events culminated in an uprising of the native servants, who killed all the remaining mutineers except Alexander Smith, who was "desperately wounded with a pistol ball in his neck." [29] The lone English survivor then allied himself with the widows of the mutineers, and in a night of slaughter they killed all the native men. Smith assumed the leadership of the colony, teaching the children (several were grown men and women when Captain Folger arrived) to read and write in the English language and instructing them in religion from the *Bounty*'s Bible.

Captain Folger left Pitcairn Island for Más Afuera, carrying away two gifts from Alexander Smith, a compass and a chronometer from the *Bounty*. Stopping first at Más a Tierra, he showed the chronometer to the Spanish commandant, who refused to return it. But the New England sealing captain retained the compass, which he later sent to the British Admiralty to verify his account of the *Bounty*'s final fate, and thus solved a mystery which he and other American seamen first pondered together on Más Afuera in 1800. Now, eight years later, Captain Folger was back at the old sealing ground, hoping to acquire a cargo of skins to offset his unsuccessful search along the coast of New Zealand. But in the intervening years, the seals and their hunters had vanished from the offshore islands and the coastal waters of Chile and Peru. Even Santa Maria was deserted, and there were no Yankee sealing captains there to hear his extraordinary tale of discovery.

8

Australasia

Captain Folger discovered the *Bounty*'s colony while sailing across the Pacific from an unsuccessful sealing expedition to the Antipodes Island, away off the southeastern coast of New Zealand. He visited the island in the hope of duplicating the enormous cargo of skins taken there a few years earlier by a sealing gang from the *Union* of New York. A ship of great venture, the *Union* was a pioneer in the waters of Australasia. The first to hunt the coasts of both Australia and New Zealand, she also reached the Fiji Islands in the earliest adventure in sandalwood attempted by a Yankee vessel. The latter expedition was organized after a shipwrecked American sailor revealed the secret of the Fijis' "Sandalwood Island" to the sealing captains at Port Jackson in New South Wales. Port Jackson was first visited by the Yankee sealers in 1792, the year the initial hunters reached the islands of the Southeastern Pacific. This was only a few years after seven hundred English convicts landed in New South Wales to begin a colony on the great southern continent then known as New Holland, the *Terra Australis incognita* of the ancient geographers.

Port Jackson, the maritime center of New South Wales, was the rendezvous for American sealing, trading, and sandalwood vessels in Australasia. For ships bound to Canton from the seal islands of the Indian Ocean and the offshore islands of Chile and Peru, and for trading vessels sailing the eastern passage to the Orient, it was a haven for rest, pleasure, provisions, and trade. However, because of the west winds that sweep the southern coast of the continent, Port Jackson often proved a difficult harbor to gain. Until the discovery of the inland passage of Bass Strait, vessels sometimes spent weeks making the port. "Thus does Port Jackson fly from us," wrote the physician of the *Ann and Hope* bound for China from Providence in 1798, "as did Italy from the wandering Trojans. A few hours of fair wind would bring us to our long wished for harbour but adverse fate and contrary winds condemn us to plow as yet the inhospitable ocean." [1] The difficulty of getting into Port Jackson was felt even more keenly by an earlier visitor from Providence, the *Mercury*, which made the port in distress, her entire ship's company stricken with scurvy. She remained ten weeks, until all her crew recovered. For other mariners, Port Jackson brought temporary freedom which ended in jail: "$1.50 cash paid to constable for searching for him [Charles Bing] when absent without leave," recorded the supercargo of the *Favourite* of Nantucket, "$3 cash paid to constable for Abraham Niles, $1 to constable for Isaac Head, $3 to constable for James Bee, $2 cash paid for jail fines for John Baptest." [2] The *Favourite* tarried at the Australasian rendezvous for over a year before departing for China in 1806 with a huge cargo of seal skins.

There were usually plenty of recruits at Port Jackson to fill, legally or illegally, the berths emptied through desertion on sealing and sandalwood vessels or on the other American ships that participated, along with the sealers, in the whiskey trade of New South Wales. This popular commerce began late in 1792, when

Captain Benjamin Page brought the *Hope* of Providence to anchor at Port Jackson. The *Hope* carried a lading of seal skins for Canton, purchased at the Falkland Islands from the American vessels hunting there, and "a small cargo of provisions and spirits for sale."[3] Her cargo included several hundred barrels of pork, beef, and flour and over seven thousand gallons of New England spirits, mainly rum. The governor of New South Wales hoped to purchase the meat and flour only, as the first visitor to his colony from America, a brigantine out of Philadelphia, had arrived a month earlier with a large cargo of wine, rum, and gin. From the latter vessel, the governor purchased less than half of the cargo, although he allowed the balance of the alcohol to be sold among the officers and soldiers in the settlement. But Captain Page did not part with the *Hope*'s food provisions until the governor's commissary also purchased the spirits. He was less successful with two of the three convicts, whose sentences of transportation had expired, that he carried in his ship to China; one tried to incite the crew to mutiny, and another went on to the captain's native Rhode Island to renew his career of crime.

The governor of New South Wales soon "lamented" the purchase of Captain Page's cargo of alcohol and credited the *Hope* with inaugurating a traffic in liquor which proved "fatal to the morals of the people."[4] The New England spirits were dispersed through the commissary to the military and civil officers of the colony, which included the superintendents who bought a large portion for resale to the convicts under their charge, although this was a complete breach of regulations. "The fondness expressed by these people for even this pernicious American spirit was incredible," observed Captain David Collins in reference to the *Hope*'s cargo; adding that many were stricken with dysentery and one man and one woman convict died as a result.[5] But even before the Providence vessel departed for Canton, liquor had become the most prized commodity in the distant and bizarre colony of New South Wales.

Official resistance to the domination of liquor in the settlement appears to have been mainly rhetorical. "Cellers," wrote the governor in 1800, "from the *better sort of people* in the colony to the darkest character among the convicts, are full of that fiery poison." [6] Yet, at the same time, the governor offered a reward of thirty gallons of spirits for the capture of two outlaws roaming the countryside. The supremacy of liquor over any other commodity or even money was established after the dispersal of the *Hope's* cargo, and henceforth it commanded more labor than provisions or articles of clothing and generally secured a better bargain than cash. Whiskey distributed through the commissary or by local merchants to the officers, soldiers, and superintendents often sold at four or five times the original price when it finally reached the free settlers and convicts. It apparently occupied a high place in the public sentiment; the governor allowed the sandalwood vessel *Eliza* of Salem to land six thousand gallons of spirits on December 21, 1805, "because of the approaching Festivals." [7]

The appearance of Yankee vessels at Port Jackson introduced a number of problems which the administrators hoped to minimize by confining the visiting ships to a special area known as Neutral Bay. The most persistent problem concerned the disposal of cargoes of alcoholic spirits, which generally entered legally through the governor's commissary or distributor or illegally through smuggling. Another difficult problem involved the desire of convicts, whose sentences of transportation had expired, to obtain berths or passage on American vessels, and a similar desire by those whose sentences had not expired. Sealing captains who had lost part of their crews through desertion on the offshore islands of Chile and Peru were particularly susceptible to this source of supply, as well as to the money obtained from smuggling convicts from the colony. Captain Amasa Delano, whose sealing expeditions along the west coast of South America and the south coast of Australia were marked by desertion, expressed his surprise a few miles clear of Neutral Bay when he "found" seventeen convicts "secreted" on his little vessel.[8]

A much publicized case of smuggling involved the *Otter* of Boston, which reached Port Jackson in 1796 from the sealing stations on the islands of St. Paul and Amsterdam in the Indian Ocean. After disposing of a cargo of rum and wine, she departed illegally with about twenty convicts, including the "Scotch Martyr," Thomas Muir. "It was reported," wrote one of Muir's fellow exiles who remained behind, "she came in here for as many of us as chose to go." [9] Ebenezer Dorr, the master of the *Otter*, put a third of the convicts ashore at Tongatabu and marooned the rest of them, except Muir, on the California coast, where they fared badly at the hands of the Spanish. Muir left the vessel earlier at Nootka Sound, transferring to a Spanish ship in the hope of reaching the United States by way of Mexico; one of the charges against him at his famous trial in Scotland for sedition was that of advocating the writings of Thomas Paine. Muir was treated decently by the Spanish, then at war with England, and put on board a ship bound from Havana to Cádiz. Shortly before reaching her destination, the Spanish vessel fell in with a British cruiser and was captured after a battle in which Muir was so severely wounded in the face that the English victors, who knew he was on board, failed to recognize him in the search. He was shipped to a hospital in Cádiz with the other wounded, and, there, the French consul secured Muir's freedom by claiming him a citizen of the Republic.

Despite widespread illegal trading and smuggling, the authorities at Port Jackson rarely used drastic measures to curtail the activities of the sealing and sandalwood vessels. Writing to London in 1802 concerning his efforts to stem the traffic in liquor and the smuggling of convicts, the governor at Port Jackson said: "It is true that the fortuitious arrival of American ships has frequently saved this colony from experiencing great want." [10] For the Yankee traders also brought to the distant settlement meat, flour, woolen and cotton goods, shoes, and tea as well as tobacco, which brought the highest price of any commodity except liquor. One of the few instances where the full extent of the law was actually used against an American ship related to the activities of the Boston sealing and sandalwood vessel *Jenny,* whose master, William Dorr, brought her to Port Jackson late in 1807, more than a decade after his brother ran the *Otter* illegally from the same port with a number of fugitives that included the "Scotch Martyr."

The *Jenny* arrived with a tempting cargo of meat and general merchandise as well as five thousand gallons of rum, wine, and brandy. However, the governor of the colony, William Bligh, refused to allow the liquor to be offered for sale through the commissary or to individuals. Captain Bligh had returned twice to the South Pacific in the eighteen years that passed since the mutiny on the *Bounty;* the first time, in 1792, when he rounded up sixteen of the mutineers still remaining at Tahiti; and again, in 1805, as governor of New South Wales. Bligh's personality, as well as his attempts to enforce the letter of the law, especially in regard to the distribution of liquor, made him an unpopular figure in the settlement; he was deposed by some of his officers early in 1808. The *Jenny,* still waiting hopefully to land her cargo of spirits, was lying at anchor directly opposite the house where Captain Bligh was deprived of his office and held under arrest. Her crew celebrated the event that evening by taking a box of candles, part of her trading cargo, and lighting up the entire ship, which the ex-governor could not avoid seeing from the adjacent windows of his confinement. However, the *Jenny*'s celebration was premature. The acting governor also refused to allow her lading of liquor to be sold, and when he heard that the Boston vessel was smuggling her cargo ashore, she was ordered out of port. She then put into Broken Bay, north of Port Jackson, and got about a fifth of her liquor ashore before she was seized by the authorities and claimed as a prize. But the court refused to decree condemnation and the *Jenny* departed for the Fijis.

At the time he was deposed, Governor Bligh was trying to curtail the advantages enjoyed by American vessels at Port Jackson and to encourage the colonists to take a more active part in the sandalwood trade at Fiji. He was continuing the policy of earlier administrators who had attempted to restrict the sealing operations of the Yankee hunters on the southern coast of Australia in favor of expeditions organized by the inhabitants of New South Wales. The master of the Boston snow *Fairy*, arriving at Port Jackson in 1793 from the hunting grounds on the islands of the Indian Ocean, was the first American to suggest that the colonists enter the sealing trade, describing the great numbers of seals he observed along the southern coast of their continent. But the New England captain, who carried three men and two women ex-convicts legitimately from the settlement, did not know that a sealing voyage had been undertaken in the *Britannia* out of Port Jackson the preceding year. The expedition hunted the islands of Dusky Bay in New Zealand for a year, taking only about forty-five hundred skins. No further expeditions were organized locally until the discovery of Bass Strait in 1798. Then, for a brief and violent time, the seal islands of this inland water were contested by American and Australian hunters.

The discovery of Bass Strait made known the large body of water separating the mainland of Australia from Tasmania, then called Van Diemen's Land. Several of the islands in the hitherto uncharted passage proved to be a habitat of the fur and hair seal. An officer on one of the first ships to sail through the strait wrote: "We passed thousands and thousands of seals, so tame, as almost to encircle the ship." [11] A few years later, the *Fanny* of Boston made the initial American run through the strait, taking more than a week to sail between the seal islands of "Kent's Group" on the east and "King's Island" on the west.[12] Her master, Eliphalet Smith, sent an account of the passage home to the

United States, where it appeared in the newspapers of New York and New England in 1803. But six months earlier, at the time Captain Smith was actually making his passage, the *Charles* cleared from Boston on a sealing expedition in which she became the first Yankee vessel to hunt the waters of Bass Strait.

Bass Strait is about two hundred miles long and approximately one hundred and fifty miles at its widest point. The sealers' activities were mainly concentrated on King Island at the western entrance and Cape Barren Island at the southeastern end. A number of sealing gangs from New South Wales were already stationed on the two islands when the first American ship ploughed through the strait late in 1802. The governor of the colony was particularly anxious to restrict the area to hunters from his settlement, as he designated the sealing trade "the most considerable among the very few natural productions of this country that can be esteemed commercial." [13] The first challenge to the sealers from Port Jackson came from a French expedition, attracted to the area by information received from the commander of the exploratory ship *Le Geographe,* sent to the South Pacific by France, which accompanied the *Fanny* in the initial American passage through the strait. When the French sealing vessel was lost off Cape Barren Island in mid-1803, the governor of New South Wales expressed his hope the disaster "may stop any more adventures from that quarter." [14] This proved to be the case; but the Yankee hunters, who arrived at the same time the French schooner was lost, were not so easily discouraged.

Less than half a dozen vessels were involved in the American sealing expeditions at Bass Strait. The initial visitor, the *Charles* of Boston, remained only a few months before her captain, James Percival, set her sails for China. The *Charles* was followed by the *Union* of New York, commanded by Isaac Pendleton and partly owned by Edmund Fanning, an early sealing captain at the Falklands and Más Afuera. Captain Pendleton brought her to the southern coast of Australia in the fall of 1803 in search of the "Seal Island" described by Captain George Vancouver in his manuscript published a few years earlier. Disappointed by the scarcity of seals in the designated area, Captain Pendleton sailed eastward to Kangaroo Island, bringing the vessel to anchor in a wide bay he named Union Harbor. The vessel rode at her cable for the few remaining months of the year, while her crew collected about fourteen thousand skins and built a schooner, which was launched as the *Independence.* The *Union* and her new tender continued the hunt on King Island before entering Port Jackson early in 1804 in quest of trade and provisions.

A month after the *Union* left King Island, at the western entrance to Bass Strait, Amasa Delano arrived from Boston in the ship *Perseverance* to keep a rendezvous with his brother, Samuel, in command of the schooner *Pilgrim.* Captain Delano, a sealing master of many years experience along the west coast of South America, was in pursuit of the prey described by the commander of the French ship of exploration that accompanied the first American vessel through the strait. His expedition carried a third brother, William Delano: "Each one of the brothers has been master builder, and master rigger, and navigator of ships and vessels in all quarters of the world." [15] Also aboard his ship *Perseverance* was Captain Delano's seven year old nephew who had lost the use of both arms, yet wanted to accompany his family on their voyage to the edge of the world. Finding few seals on King Island, they ran down to Cape Barren Island, at the eastern end of the strait, where they discovered six gangs hunting among the islets and rocks.

The two Boston vessels lay off Cape Barren Island for almost eight months despite the presence of the rival hunters, mainly convicts from Port Jackson whose sentences of transportation had not expired. With their common prey none too plentiful, the competitors from New England and old England were soon at war. A long series of raids, brawls, and kidnappings ended in a final attack on one of the Australian camps by the New Englanders just before they sailed. Dragging the master of the gang and four of his men into the woods, the Yankees tied them to trees and flogged them with a cat-o'-nine-tails. When the Australian leader succeeded in getting free, he was chased into the water by one of Captain Delano's men and severely beaten with a club; the punishment only ended when a number of other Englishmen were attracted to the scene by the cries of their comrades. Despite the Americans' final act of vengeance, more than a dozen of the convict and ex-convict rival sealers deserted to the New England vessels when they departed from the embattled hunting ground.

The administrators of New South Wales had, hitherto, lacked sufficient reasons to restrict legally the activities of the American sealers in the colony. But the launching of a forty-ton schooner by the crew of the *Union* at Kangaroo Island, the clashes between the competing hunters in Bass Strait, and the smuggling of so many men into the vessels commanded by the Delano brothers brought into question the maintenance of security in the penal settlement. The governor found enough support to issue a proclamation barring all English subjects from berths on American sealing and trading ships, and prohibiting the construction of any vessel with a keel over fourteen feet, or the construction, by foreigners, of any buildings or shelters on the islands and bays of the colony. The restrictions against the sealers came too late. The Delano's expedition to Bass Strait was the last serious American attempt to hunt the southern coast of Australia, while the *Union* had already departed in search of the seal island "placed on some ancient charts, and said to have been discovered by Tasman" that brought the final phase of sealing in Australasia to the southern tip of New Zealand.[16]

The *Union*'s quest brought her to the Antipodes Island, a remote habitat of the fur seal on the edge of the Southern Ocean. The vessel lay on and off the island while Captain Pendleton put a gang of twelve men ashore to hunt for a year's period. The *Union* then returned to New South Wales where her master formed a strange partnership with one of the leading merchants of the colony. Their object was to organize an adventure to one of the Fiji Islands, for the great topic of conversation among the shipmasters and merchants at Port Jackson in the summer of 1804 was the discovery of sandalwood at Vanua Levu and the recognition of its importance as a trading commodity at Canton. The news of the existence of sandalwood at Vanua Levu—the "Great Land" of Fiji—had been spread by an American seaman, Oliver Slater, a survivor of the wreck of the *Argo*.

The *Argo*, a small schooner flying the Stars and Stripes, arrived at Port Jackson from Mauritius in mid-1798 with a cargo of salt provisions and brandy.[17] She sailed for China early in October on an unusual course between the Fijis and Tonga and, apparently veering too far west, struck at night on the Bukatatanoa Reefs and became a total wreck. The next morning, the natives of Lakemba, about ten miles away, paddled over to the site of the wreck—the reefs and sunken rocks enclosing the lagoon are now called Argo Reefs—where they met with a strange sight: "Though they resemble men, yet they are spirits, for their ears are bound up with scarlet, and they bit burning wood." [18] The crew of the *Argo*, wearing red woolen caps and smoking pipes, were among the first Westerners to set foot on the Fiji Islands.

The survivors of the *Argo* were first taken to nearby Lakemba and Oneata, and later reached the larger islands of Fiji and Tonga. Most of them apparently shared the fate of future American and English seamen who were wrecked at the Fijis or who deserted there from sandalwood vessels over the next decade: they joined in the local wars and met violent deaths. Captain Samuel Chase of the Nantucket whaler *Harriet* picked up a seaman at Tongatabu who claimed to be a survivor of the *Argo* and recounted how the master and some of his crew perished in the civil wars raging at Tonga. The wreck of the *Argo*, which indirectly introduced the sandalwood trade to the sealing captains and traders at Port Jackson, decisively changed the history of Fiji. The survivors of the little schooner brought gunpowder and cholera to the islands. Cholera is first recorded at Vanua Levu—the Yankees' "Sandalwood Island"—after the wreck of the *Argo*, when the king's death from "the Foreign Disease" was followed by a great storm of hailstones which his subjects thought were falling stars as they melted in their hands.[19] One of their sagas recounts the effects of the disease which decimated the populations of large sections of the island:

> The great sickness sits aloft,
> Their voices sound hoarsely.
> They fall and lie helpless and pitiable,
>
> . . .
>
> The *likn* * knotted round them they do not loose,
> Hark to the creak of the strangling-cords.
> The spirits flow away like running water, *ra taw e*.[20]

Two years after the wreck of the *Argo*, one of the survivors, Oliver Slater, was rescued by the ship *El Plumier* out of Port Jackson. Partly owned by Thomas Palmer, one of the "Scotch Martyrs" who chose to remain at New South Wales, the vessel set out in 1801 in search of *bêche-de-mer*. Stopping for provisions at Tongatabu, her master heard of the trade in sandalwood between the natives of Tonga and Vanua Levu, and decided to try to reach the unknown and uncharted Fiji Islands and acquire there a cargo far more valuable at Canton than *bêche-de-mer*. He managed to get his ship into the Koro Sea, where he discovered Oliver Slater on one of the islands. The rescued American seaman guided the vessel into the harbor of Mbua, on Vanua Levu, the future "Sandalwood Bay." The traders from Port Jackson obtained fifteen tons of sandalwood for an assortment of knives, hatchets, and other pieces of iron. *El Plumier*, which originally sailed under Spanish colors and was captured by the English and sold as a prize ship to her present owners at New South Wales, was well on the way to China when she was recaptured by the Spanish and made a prize at Guam.

Although judged prisoners of war, the crew of *El Plumier* were well treated by the Spanish. Thomas Palmer died shortly

* The cord used to strangle the victims of cholera to prevent their spreading the disease.

after the condemnation of his vessel, but Oliver Slater and one of the other owners, John Boston, removed from Guam to the Philippines, where the latter operated a large distillery at Manila. There, they met an English merchant-trader, J.E. Farrell, owner of the ship *Fair American,* who was extremely interested in their account of the sandalwood trade at the Fijis. They planned an expedition to Vanua Levu with Captain Farrell commander of the vessel, John Boston supercargo, and Oliver Slater guide and interpreter. Departing together from the Philippines in the *Fair American,* they reached New South Wales in the spring of 1804. The governor of the colony described the vessel as "a ship of 300 tons, under American colours . . . The pretext was that she was bringing cattle, of which *two* arrived, but a considerable object was 7,203 *gallons of spirits.*" [21] Boston, a distiller in England before emigrating to the penal settlement as a free subject, was responsible for the cargo, which was about two-thirds rum and one-third gin.

Oliver Slater left the *Fair American* at Port Jackson to enter the service of another free settler who had sailed in command of local vessels since the first years of the colony and was now entering the sandalwood trade. John Boston and Simeon Lord, an ex-convict who had become one of the leading merchants of New South Wales, then formed the partnership with Captain Pendleton of the *Union,* which the governor of the colony branded "an errant fraud on the Americn owners of the vessel." [22] Captain Pendleton sold the fourteen thousand seal skins his crew took at Bass Strait to Lord and Boston on credit, to be paid out of the profits from a cargo of sandalwood taken at the Fijis and sold in China. The balance of the profits from the sandalwood expedition was to finance the purchase of a ship in the United States that would return to Port Jackson and be operated there for the advantages of the partners. Captain Farrell also joined in the adventure; his ship *Fair American* was to rendezvous with the *Union* at Tongatabu and from there the two vessels would sail for Vanua Levu.

The *Union* reached Tongatabu, the largest of the group Captain Cook named the Friendly Islands, at the end of September 1804. Captain Pendleton anchored his vessel at Nukualofa, where he hoped to take on a native Tongan who knew the dialect of Vanua Levu to act as guide and interpreter. The following morning, a number of natives in canoes paddled out to the vessel and their leader, a Malayan who spoke English, informed the master there was wood, water, and provisions available on shore for trade. Captain Pendleton and his new supercargo, John Boston, and six men armed with guns and cutlasses set out for shore in a small boat. After the captain left the ship, many of the natives scrambled aboard to trade, but when they began passing up war clubs from the canoes below, the chief mate ordered them from the vessel. He also fired a gun to warn the crew on shore, as he saw through his glass that the vessel's small boat was lying broadside on. The next day passed anxiously, with no word from the shore; but on the third day, the English-speaking Malayan returned, bringing a white woman in the canoe among the natives. Both told the mate the captain wanted him ashore, although, when unobserved by the Malayan, the woman seemed to signal a warning to the Yankee crew. They returned the following morning, and again urged the mate to come ashore. But, suddenly, the white woman stood up, shouted that the mariners who landed had been massacred, and jumped from her canoe into the water. The men on the *Union* fired their guns around her to keep the natives away, and finally got her on shipboard.

The woman, whose name was Elizabeth Morey, told the mate that as soon as the master, supercargo, and the six sailors from the *Union* landed, they were taken out of sight and all but two immediately killed. From the seamen whose lives were temporarily spared, she learned what ship it was; she also learned that the native chief, Teoo Cava, intended to capture it. "Malay Charley" was sent first, alone with the natives, to entice the mate and more of the crew ashore, but when he failed, she was ordered to help in the effort, as the Tongan chief believed the vessel was still too well-manned to be easily taken. She told how the two survivors from the landing party had been killed, and of her own attempts to warn the crew the previous day. When she finished her story, the mate, now in full command, ordered the men to fire upon the natives who were circling the ship in their canoes. Then the anchor cables were cut and the vessel put out to sea.

Elizabeth Morey told the men of the *Union* the story of the capture of an American ship at Nukualofa several years earlier, and the massacre of some of the crew, which ended in her own plight as the wife of the Tongan chief Teoo Cava. She arrived at the Friendly Islands in the summer of 1802 with Captain Lovat Mellon of the former Boston ship *Duke of Portland.* Captain Mellon had originally sailed from the Philippines in command of a brig belonging to the American consul at Manila, but when he reached his destination at Batavia, he violated his trust, selling both cargo and vessel, and with the proceeds purchased his own ship. In this vessel, the *Duke of Portland,* Captain Mellon traded at various ports before reaching Cape Town, where he took Elizabeth Morey aboard as his companion. The *Duke of Portland,* flying American colors, rounded the Australian continent into the Tasman Sea, where she touched at Norfolk Island. At this remote spot, administered as part of the penal settlement of New South Wales, the master smuggled a number of convicts on board and then headed his vessel north across the Tropic of Capricorn in the direction of Fiji and Tonga.

Anchoring off the island of Tongatabu, Captain Mellon was hailed by a white man named Doyle, believed to be a survivor of the *Argo.* One of the first of the dangerous American and English beachcombers wrecked or deserting on the islands of Tonga and Fiji, Doyle planned the capture of the *Duke of Portland.* Enticing the second mate and eight sailors ashore in one of the small boats, he sent the mate back with a request for two more boatloads of men. His request was granted, reducing the number on board to the captain, the first officer, Elizabeth Morey, her Negro woman servant, and nine seamen. Doyle returned with the small boats and a number of natives who swarmed aboard and got control of the ship. They killed the master and mate, and seven of the crew, throwing their bodies overboard, but they spared the lives of Elizabeth Morey, her servant, and two seamen. Taken ashore, the survivors learned that all but three of the crew landed in the small boats had perished in a similar massacre. Doyle and the natives worked for several days unloading the vessel, but needing the assistance of the five surviving seamen to complete the task, brought them aboard. However, once back on their ship, the seamen turned upon their captors, killed Doyle, and drove the natives over the sides. They put the *Duke of Portland* to sea, leaving Elizabeth Morey at Nukualofa, where she remained as one of the wives of the chief until her rescue by the *Union*. Her Negro servant is described by an English captive at Tonga, almost a decade later, as insane but living in the house of a female chieftain who treated her with great kindness.

The new master of the *Union,* former mate Daniel Wright, took the vessel back to Port Jackson where he hoped to replace the eight members of the crew killed at Tongatabu. He was allowed to advertise in the local paper for replacements only from among the Yankee mariners in the settlement: "The Commander of the ship "Union" being in distress . . . desires Americans in this Port forthwith to apply to him, when they will immediately receive a Bounty on Entering, and meet such suitable encouragement as they shall merit." [23] The notice appeared in the same issue of the Port Jackson newspaper which describes the massacre of part of the ship's crew at Nukualofa. With only a few recruits, the *Union* sailed for the Fijis late in 1804. Her master still expected to obtain the cargo of sandalwood whose sale at Canton would expedite the completion of the other terms in the contract between the New South Wales merchant Simeon Lord and the vessel's captain and supercargo who perished in the massacre at Tonga. The *Union* was almost in sight of Sandalwood Bay, on Vanua Levu, when she struck a reef in a heavy gale. The vessel broke up with most of her crew drowning among the wreckage. The survivors were slaughtered by the natives of Koro

Island, who had watched the destruction from the shore and raced to the scene in their canoes.

An officer of the *Union* and eight members of the ship's company were skinning seals far away on the Antipodes Island when the vessel was wrecked on the reefs in the Koro Sea. They had been on their lonely hunting ground almost a year before Simeon Lord at Port Jackson learned of the destruction in the Fijis of their ship. The death of both masters and the supercargo left him in sole possession of the fourteen thousand skins taken earlier by the crew of the vessel at Bass Strait. He had the responsibility of getting the men off the distant seal island, but he also had the prospect of owning the cargo they obtained there, although he did not dream they had stacked sixty thousand pelts. Yet this was the rich harvest of skins that descended to Simeon Lord, who is described by the governor of New South Wales as one of the "*Vipers* which this Colony possesses."[24] When the *Union*'s tender made Port Jackson in mid-1805, Lord sent her and the *Favourite* of Nantucket to relieve the men on the Antipodes. The huge cargo of skins was stowed in the *Favourite* and the hunters and the rescue vessels departed for Port Jackson. The tender was lost in a storm on the way back, the final disaster in the annals of the *Union*.

The *Union*'s ill-starred adventures more or less marked the ending of one American activity in Australasia—sealing—and the opening of another—the sandalwood trade. For despite the destruction of the *Union* on the reefs in the Koro Sea, her sister ship, the *Fair American*, went on to Vanua Levu and became the first vessel flying the Stars and Stripes to arrive at Canton with a cargo of sandalwood from Fiji. And for about half a dozen years, between 1805 and 1812, a number of sealing and trading ships out of New England and New York made their way cautiously through the reef-infested waters to Sandalwood Island. It was a very different world from the solitary, wind-swept hunting grounds of the southern oceans, where the only sounds were the surf smashing against the rocks, the call of the sea birds, and the mournful cry of the seals.

9

Fiji

The Fiji Islands were uncharted and practically unknown when the first Yankee vessels reached the northern side of Vanua Levu, where the redolent sandalwood grew on the high hills beyond the barrier reefs. More than a century and an half earlier, the Dutch navigator Abel Tasman, probably the earliest Westerner to drift among the shoals and breakers of Fiji, sighted the eastern outlying islets of Vanua Levu. Captain Cook, who sailed along the most southern island on his last voyage of discovery, heard of the existence of "Feejee" during his sojourn at the neighboring islands of Tonga. But it was Cook's sailing master, William Bligh, the future commander of the *Bounty,* who was the real pioneer in the waters of Fiji. And at the time the initial American vessel reached Sandalwood Island, the archipelago of Fiji was also known as Bligh's Islands.

William Bligh held the commission of lieutenant when he took the *Bounty* on her tumultous voyage to Polynesia in quest of the breadfruit tree. When part of the crew mutinied in 1789 off Tongatabu, Bligh and his loyal officers and men were set adrift in the vessel's open launch and began a thirty-six-hundred-mile trek across the South Pacific to Timor. Their path carried them through the Koro Sea, past the islands and reefs separating Vanua Levu and Viti Levu, and out to the western-most of the Fiji Islands, where Lieutenant Bligh saw two large canoes with many armed men coming toward them "and being apprehensive of their intentions, we rowed with some anxiety, fully conscious of our weak and defenseless state." [1] Bligh returned to the South Pacific in 1792, again in quest of the bread-fruit tree, and in search of the mutineers of the *Bounty*. His track took him back through the Koro Sea, in the wake of the islands he had described on his first, anxious passage. Seven years later, the *Ann and Hope*, bound to China from Providence, coasted along the southern and western islands of Fiji. "Capt. Cook," noted a passenger aboard the vessel, "did not proceed to explore them and it is possible that we are the first whites who have seen them." [2]

But at least three vessels had penetrated the reefs along the eastern perimeter of Fiji in the half dozen years after Bligh returned to the islands in 1792. The passenger on the Rhode Island ship did not know that an American sailor, a survivor from the *Argo*, was then living on one of the islands in the Koro Sea, and that two years later he would guide the first vessel to the sandal-wood hills of Vanua Levu. Vanua Levu—the Great Land—is the second largest of the Fiji Islands, about a hundred miles long and thirty miles at its widest point. Like the other islands of the archipelago, it is of volcanic origin with sharp contours and lofty hills covered with rich vegetation. The early traders described the great beauty of Vanua Levu at the beginning of the nineteenth century, when sandalwood still grew above the bays along the northwestern shore of the island. It was the lure of this parasitic tree—*Santalum yasi*—that drew a dozen sealing and trading captains from New York and New England to Vanua Levu to participate in the most daring and dangerous of the adventures to China.

Long before the Yankees reached the islands, the natives of Tonga established a trade in sandalwood with their neighbors on Fiji, crossing the hundred or so miles of ocean in open canoes. The aromatic oil of the sandalwood tree was prized in Polynesia for scenting coconut oil used as a body ointment. The Tongans first bartered with bark cloth and the sting of the ray, but by the end of the eighteenth century, whale teeth had become the most valuable item of trade. Whales' teeth were so highly valued at the time the sandalwood traders reached Vanua Levu that if a white man were known to have one, "the axe, or the club, on some unlucky occasion, would deprive him of it for ever, and of his life too." [3] The Fijians called the whale the "Fish for Teeth," and originally relied on the supply brought from Tonga, where the sperm whale—the Cacholot—frequented the outlying waters. But when Tonga became a rendezvous for American and English vessels in the South Pacific, especially whaling ships, a larger supply became available for barter at Vanua Levu. The Fijians preferred old, red-colored teeth to newer, white ones; when the Yankee trading captains reached Sandalwood Island, they set their men to work making them out of odd pieces of ivory and applying various stains.

The American sandalwood expeditions were organized at Port Jackson by sealing captains who arrived there from the hunting grounds of the southern oceans or in New York, Boston, and Salem by merchants and captains whose vessels usually made their first landfall along the southern coast of Australia. After disposing of their trading cargoes at the principal harbor in New South Wales—ladings mainly composed of rum, gin, brandy, and wine—they went on to Tongatabu, the largest of the islands in the Tonga group. Captain Cook had named them the Friendly Islands "as a firm alliance and friendship seems to subsist among their inhabitants, and their courteous behaviour to strangers intitles them to that appellation." [4] By the time the Yankee traders reached Tongatabu—the Sacred Tonga—the spirit of friendship and courtesy honored by Captain Cook had deteriorated through the influence of the "beachcombers," men who deserted or were discharged there from American and English ships.

One early group of beachcombers arrived in the Boston sealing vessel *Otter,* which ran illegally from Port Jackson in 1796 with about twenty convicts smuggled aboard. Her captain left half a dozen of the convicts behind at Tongatabu, as well as several sealers who had signed on the vessel at the home port in America. The first English missionaries, who reached Tonga the following year, were far more afraid of the beachcombers than of the natives. The beachcombers, participating in the civil wars, tried to enhance their position with the local chiefs by planning the destruction of trading vessels like the *Duke of York* and the *Union,* in order to obtain guns and supplies. They were largely responsible for the Tongans' becoming stigmatized at this time as "a nation of wreckers." [5] Although the mortality rate among the beachcombers was high, there was a constant supply from deserters and discharged sailors at both Tongatabu and Sandalwood Island. Twenty-six were added to their ranks when the English ship *Port au Prince* was captured at Tonga in 1806 with the loss of twenty-two seamen. Yet some of the survivors of this disaster, who went to the smaller islands free from the influence of the beachcombers, found that the natives there well deserved the "appellation" Captain Cook bestowed upon them three decades earlier.

Tongatabu was relatively well-known when the Spanish prize ship *El Plumier,* sailing out of Port Jackson under English colors, reached the island in 1801 and her master heard about the sandalwood trade between the natives of Tonga and Fiji. He took the ship to the Fiji Islands, then almost unknown to American and English mariners, discovered Oliver Slater on one of the islands, and was guided by this survivor of the *Argo* to Vanua Levu. *El Plumier* obtained the first cargo of sandalwood for the Canton market, although the ship never reached her destination, being recaptured by the Spanish off Guam. But several years later, when Oliver Slater and some of her crew got back to Port Jackson, they spread the secret of Vanua Levu. The sandalwood race began late in 1804, when the *Union* sailed on her ill-fated voyage to Tonga and Fiji. Despite the attack on the *Union* at Nukualofa and her wreck on the reefs of Fiji, the future American sandalwood expeditions followed her track from Port Jackson to Tongatabu and from there through the Koro Sea to Vanua Levu.

The ninety-ton *Union,* mounting four guns and carrying a crew of twenty-two, was not the model for the American ships in the sandalwood trade. Of the dozen vessels from New York and New England that reached Vanua Levu between 1805 and 1812, the average burden was two hundred and thirty-three tons, six guns, and a crew of twenty-two. When the owners of the *Union* sent their first vessel, the *Hope,* direct from America to Sandalwood Island, her tonnage and armaments were double those of the pioneering vessel, and she carried a crew of twenty-six. The second ship the company sent out from New York, the *Tonquin,* was three hundred tons burden and pierced with twenty-two guns. The two-hundred-and-five-ton *Jenny,* a sealing vessel out of Boston carrying fourteen men and six guns, arrived at New South Wales in 1807 with the following orders: "If any thing promising or informing turns up at Port Jackson, sufficient to induce going to New Zealand, and to any Islands for procuring Sandal Wood . . . you are at liberty to pursue it." [6] Her voyage, so far, had been a losing one; she had failed to obtain a cargo of seal skins and had been driven from Port Jackson for illegal trading. Her master, deciding to enter the sandalwood trade, prepared for the more dangerous adventure by taking on three additional seamen at New South Wales and increasing the armaments by two swivel guns and ten muskets.

The onetime sealing captain Edmund Fanning, one of the owners of the *Union,* directed the master of the company's next vessel in the sandalwood trade to obtain information relating to the massacre of the captain, supercargo, and six sailors from the

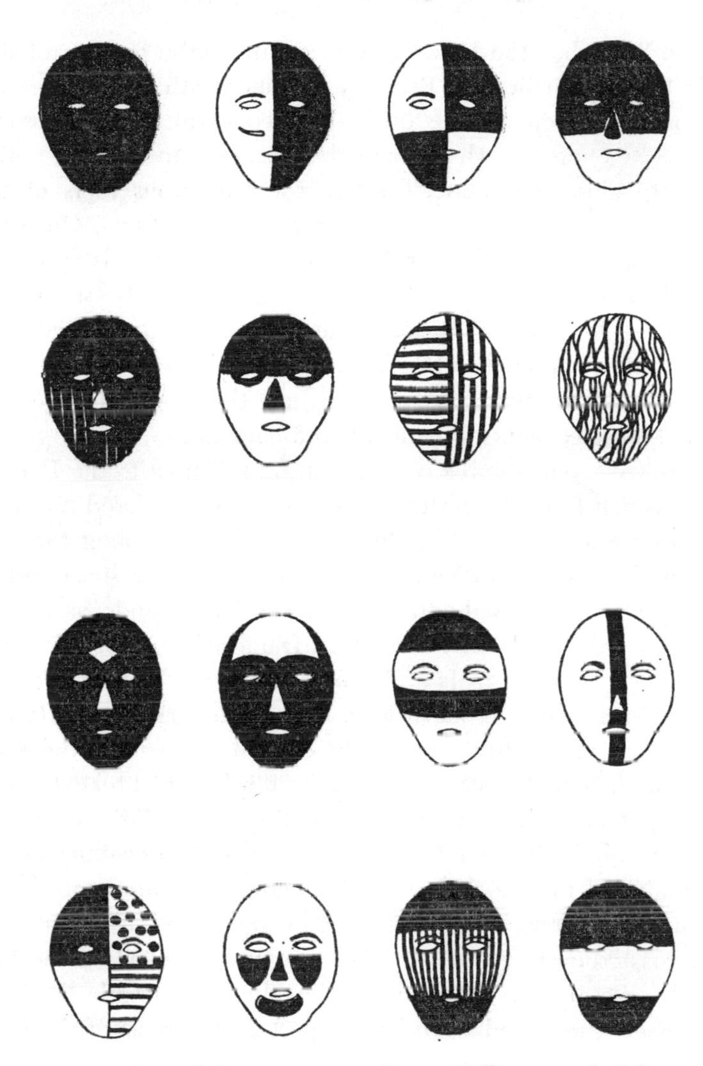

Fijian modes of face painting. From Williams and Calvert, *Fiji and the Fijians* (London, 1859).

Union. Yet, when the *Hope* arrived at Tongatabu on this mission in 1807, Captain Reuben Brumley was met with total silence on the part of whomever he questioned concerning the massacre three years earlier. He managed, however, to hire a native Fijian to guide the vessel through the dangerous reefs of the Koro Sea and to act as an interpreter at Vanua Levu. Once the Americans established their bases on Sandalwood Island, and gained some knowledge of the Koro Sea, it was less essential to secure a guide and an interpreter at Tonga. But the sandalwood traders still continued to break the passage from Port Jackson to the Fijis with a stop at Tongatabu, where they took on large supplies of hogs, coconuts, breadfruit, and bananas.

The voyage across the open ocean from Tonga to the Lau Islands, which form the eastern perimeter of Fiji, offered no problems to the Yankee vessels. But once entangled among the Lau Islands, the passage to Vanua Levu, at the northwestern end of the Koro Sea, was filled with danger. The Lau Islands, as well as the principal islands on the western fringe of the Koro Sea, are surrounded by coral reefs and shoals which made navigation by sailing ships extremely hazardous. The missionary ship *Duff*, one of the early vessels to penetrate the eastern barrier into the Koro Sea, struck a reef over which the water hardly broke to give warning. One of her passengers, mindful of the Fijians' reputation for cannibalism, wrote of the general fear prevailing as the crew labored to free the vessel: "Imagination, quick and fertile on such occasions, figured them dancing round us, while we were roasted on large fires." [7] The *Argo* was wrecked on the Lau Islands several years later, and within the next decade the Yankee vessels *Union* and *Eliza* broke apart on the reefs of the Koro Sea.

Reefs and shoals were not the only hazards that confronted the sandalwood vessels as they maneuvered cautiously across the uncharted sea from the Lau Islands to Vanua Levu. The *Hope* of New York, entering the Koro Sea in mid-1807, took three anxious weeks to reach Sandalwood Island, during which time the

Fijian guide taken on at Tonga deserted and the vessel was attacked by natives. Four large double sailing canoes, each carrying about a hundred men armed with spears, clubs, and bows, streamed out from an island to the vessel, which then had only nineteen seamen aboard since the mate and six sailors had gone ahead in the whale boat to find a channel through the reefs into Sandalwood Bay. One of the native boats tried to close under the ship's stern and make her fast; the three other canoes kept circling round and round, making a tremendous noise to divert the crew. They kept it up for several hours, while the captain had his men stationed at the guns "loaded with round shot and matches burning."[8] The natives finally sailed away, shaking their spears and clubs at the Yankees.

After the passage through the Koro Sea, the trading vessels came to rest at Sandy Hook (Lekumbi Point). Sandy Hook formed one side of the entrance to Sandalwood Bay (Mbua Bay), which the vessels entered through Union Passage, named for the pioneering New York ship. The first cargoes were cut from the hills in the vicinity of Sandalwood Bay, under the protection of the friendly chief—or king, as he was often called—of Mbua. When this supply was exhausted, the traders moved further along the northern shore of Vanua Levu to Wailea Bay, where the Yankees made their headquarters on Brown's Island (Ngalo Island). Wailea was the main area of activity as long as the Americans continued in the sandalwood trade, until early in 1812; although when the second New York vessel in the sandalwood trade named *Hope* reached Brown's Island in 1810, she was described as having "no prospect whatever of obtaining any wood, which appears to have been entirely cut down."[9] The most eastern limit of the sandalwood country was Nanduri Bay, where the operational center was the island of Mathuata, known as Mudwater by the Yankee sailors.

The first American cargoes of sandalwood were gathered from the hills behind Mbua, the principal town on Sandalwood Bay. The chief or king of Mbua, Tui Na Mbouwalu, extended friendship and co-operation to the traders, which was essential to the success of the adventure since all the trees in each of the four domains of the sandalwood country were traditionally the property of its ruling chief. When the trading vessels passed Sandy Hook and came to anchor in the wide bay, whose black sandy shore was lined with coconut trees, the chief always came aboard to greet the captain. There was an exchange of gifts; the captain gave a selection of glittering trinkets and the ruler of Mbua offered a hog, fish, yams, and coconuts. The initial greeting between a Fijian chief and a ship's master was highly ceremonial, although one New England trader failed to maintain the dignity implied in the ceremony. The captain of the sealing ship *Jenny* was first welcomed to Fiji by a chief whose wife gravely placed in his arms a large baked shark, folded in green leaves and piping hot. The odor from the steaming fish was so strong the captain released his hold on it in order to cover his nostrils. The huge fish broke into pieces on the deck with a smell that drove the master to his cabin, from whence he refused to emerge to accept the pieces the chief's wife held out to him. Although she was greatly offended, the gift of a mirror and a handful of beads appeared to repair the damage.

After the chief and the ship's master exchanged greetings, and trade in food and provisions was opened with the natives, a treaty was generally signed specifying the amount of sandalwood that could be obtained and the conditions for cutting and carrying the cargo to the vessel. The king of Mbua ratified the treaty by presenting the trading captains with a large green branch. Tui Na Mbouwalu's good will toward the Americans contributed strongly to the safety and profits of the adventures at Sandalwood Bay and the early ones at Wailea, whose ruler was less powerful than the king of Mbua. The *Hope* of New York acquired a fine cargo at Sandalwood Bay with a minimum of difficulties, largely through the friendship between the ruler and the vessel's first mate, for whom Brown's Island at Wailea Bay was named. Brown lived with the chief's family, was treated as an adopted son, and learned the Fijian language. When his vessel departed for Canton in mid-1807, Brown promised to return in another of the company's ships within "eighteen moons." He kept his word, arriving at Sandalwood Bay in the *Tonquin* at the end of 1808: "The King instantly encircled him in his arms, as if a child, when one minute passed, and another, and yet another —His Majesty seemingly too much absorbed by his feelings to be willing to slack up his embrace—with the continued expressions, 'My son! My son!' The large, pearly drops rolled down his cheeks, and he was, to all appearance quite overjoyed, and affectionately unmanned in again meeting with his adopted son! This scene seemed, apparently, not only to petrify our officers and men, as they gazed on it, but also the natives, fixing them, like statues, on the deck." [10]

The scrubby sandalwood trees were felled in the hills by a gang of natives, about fifty in number, under the supervision of a lesser chief who shared with the king in the distribution of the trading articles. The natives cut down the trees designated by a member of the ship's crew, who had to be able to distinguish between the genuine *Santalum yasi* and a similar tree which quickly lost its fragrance and had no value at Canton. A decade earlier, a New York sealing captain had carried a cargo of the spurious wood from Hawaii to China where it was pronounced valueless and thrown into the river that leads to the trading capital at Canton. The seaman in charge selected the older trees which were cut as close to the ground as possible since the butt, or bottom, of the mature tree has the highest concentration of oil. The ship's officer or crew member in charge of the cutting detail also had the responsibility of safeguarding the axes and saws used by the natives who found in these tools an enormous temptation for theft.

There was much competiton among the Fijian woodcutters for positions on the cross, or two-man, saw "owing to the exquisite and delightful music, to them, in the ringing of the saw." [11] After the tree was cut down at the butt, the top was lopped off, the limbs removed, and the bark and sap shaved off, leaving only the fragrant heartwood of the scrub. It took several days for the gang to hew and trim the number of trees that could be carried on their shoulders as they marched single file through the hills to the beach. Here, the ship's crew and a number of Fijians sawed the trunks and the limbs into lengths of four or five feet. The Yankee traders at Sandalwood Bay, and later at Wailea Bay, built a hut on the beach where the wood was stored. When the amount of wood specified in the treaty was obtained, the chief had it carried to the ship in canoes and claimed his share of the trading articles.

The most persuasive article of trade was the whale's tooth, which was invested with a wide range of material and magical values. The Fijians wore a whale's tooth around their necks on important occasions, gave them as a daughter's dowry at marriage, used them to secure alliances and other forms of help, and to propitiate their gods. A genuine whale's tooth averaged about one pound in weight, although counterfeits were bartered during the sandalwood boom, made into various sizes from the ivory of the elephant's tusk. The tooth was usually presented for trade in a highly polished state with a small hole through the larger end so it could be suspended from a ribbon or cord. The Fijians wore other ornaments around their necks and arms, and in their ears. An American sailor, wrecked in the *Eliza* on a reef in the Koro Sea in 1808, begged the natives to return his protection papers, which they found in his hat, "but they took the papers and rolled them up and put them thro' the holes in the rims of their ears and wore them off." [12] The blade of the adze, hatchet, and ax was the most valued barter after the whale's tooth, followed by glass bottles, colored calico, small mirrors, beads, shining metal buttons, and, finally, needles, iron spikes, and nails.

The master of the *Hope* of New York, one of the early vessels to complete an adventure for China at Sandalwood Bay, rewarded the ruler with a chest filled with bright trinkets, cottons, and iron ware. He had the ship's carpenter make the chest fourteen feet long, divide it into a number of compartments with separate lids, and provided padlocks for each compartment which the king alone was taught to operate. The chest was painted in gaudy colors, and when all the compartments were filled, the keys, tied together by silk and beaded ribbons, were presented to the ruler in a formal ceremony. The captain estimates the cost of the articles in the United States at nine hundred dollars while the cargo yielded a hundred times that much in trade at Canton. Still, the visiting captains could not always profit from the Fijians concept of trade; the chief at Wailea tried unsuccessfully to barter for the first group of white women who arrived at Vanua Levu. They were English missionaries taken off Tahiti by a Port Jackson sandalwood vessel which struck a reef near Brown's Island late in 1809. Fortunately for them, a New York vessel was trading there at the time and gave them assistance and protection. Finding that the Yankee seamen worked on Sunday, the missionaries were disturbed although "they bear it in silence." [13] Their women were given a refuge on the American ship while their own vessel was repaired and her master from Port Jackson bartered, with other goods, for sandalwood.

When Captain Pendleton of the *Union* attempted the first American adventure in sandalwood, he was in partnership with two of the leading merchants of New South Wales, and for the next decade, until 1814, trading captains out of Port Jackson competed in Fiji, in more or less equal numbers, with those of the United States. In fact, the masters of colonial vessels from the Australian continent vainly attempted to monopolize the trade, contending that Fiji lay within the jurisdiction of the governor of New South Wales. The Yankees never accepted this interpretation, which occasionally led to fights among the rival crews, similar to the earlier conflicts between American and Australian sealing gangs at Bass Strait. The colonial vessels, which could not legally contest the monopoly of the East India Company's trade with China, generally carried their cargoes back to

Port Jackson. Sometimes, an American ship acquired sandalwood at New South Wales before starting the passage to Vanua Levu, although this was an expensive way of obtaining part of a cargo by a vessel that was actually going, herself, to Fiji.

In the first three years of the sandalwood trade, between 1805 and the outbreak of civil war on Vanua Levu in 1808, the natives were hospitable and friendly to the visiting seamen from the five American vessels that obtained cargoes there for the Canton market. "Their disposition," wrote William Lockerby, "is mild and generous and their affection toward their relations seldom found among Europeans." [14] Lockerby, first mate on the *Jenny* of Boston, remained on at Sandalwood Bay for almost a year after his vessel departed for China in 1808. Like another first officer, Brown of the *Hope* and the *Tonquin,* he lived with the chief's family, learned the language, and was honored as a chief by being fed by one of the natives. Lockerby, who took a Fijian wife, described the custom of strangling the wife, or wives, of a deceased man. The widow sat on the edge of the grave, her feet upon the body of her dead husband; a rope was twisted round her neck and pulled tightly by a man at each end; another man covered her eyes, while a woman held her feet together; her hands were left loose.

The Fijians' indulgence in cannibalism was a more lively concern to the sandalwood traders than their custom of strangling widows on husbands' graves. Yet all the early visitors admit the Fijians ate only the flesh of prisoners taken in battle, and Lockerby saw no instance of cannibalism in the first nine months he lived among them. Cannibalism apparently became uncontrolled, and largely separated from its religious context, after 1808, when the American and English trading crews and the beachcombers joined in the local wars, introducing guns and cannon which accounted for tremendously increased casualties. The traders and beachcombers, present at the victory feasts when the limbs and bodies of the vanquished were roasted, did not knowingly participate in the ritual. However, Lockerby notes: "Some of my companions, I am sorry to say, eat [sic] a part of it involuntarily, mistaking it for pork, as it was cooked, and resembled it very much."[15] The master of a Port Jackson vessel, who assisted the ruler at Nanduri Bay with men and guns, was rewarded, after the victorious battle, with an entire body freshly cooked on hot stones; the captain had his men throw it overboard.

The white man's guns brought a new and terrible force to the Fijis. The veteran sealing captain Edmund Fanning, who sent two successful adventures to Vanua Levu, affirmed "in all voyages of traffic with these children of nature, he has ever insisted that when fire-arms, powder, and ball, with other of the civilized destructive instruments of war, were demanded and peremptorily insisted on by the chiefs, in barter, to quit the trade sooner than comply; as there is no doubt that these, to them new and destructive instruments, after they and their neighbors have come into possession of some of them, have been the cause of much bloodshed and massacre."[16] The trading captains prohibited a barter in arms because their fragile superiority over the natives was due to a monopoly of firearms and the ability to use them. At the same time, the early traders showed restraint in their own use of guns, as the success of the venture depended upon the co-operation of the chief and the lesser rulers. The situation changed in mid-1808 when other rulers on Vanua Levu, adjacent to the sandalwood country, demanded a share in the wealth accumulated so unexpectedly by the chief at Mbua through barter with the trading captains.

The friendly ruler of Mbua had accumulated a great treasury of whale teeth, iron implements, mirrors, calicoes, and beads and buttons. At a ceremony in 1807, when he and a Yankee ship's master signed a treaty on a lawn under the branches of the breadfruit tree, the chief was hailed by his people as the richest monarch in the world. However, he did not wish to share his wealth with other rulers of the island who did not possess dominion over the sandalwood forests. And when these chiefs began attacking and harassing his people and his allies in the area around Wailea Bay, where the cargoes for several vessels were being gathered in the hills, he appealed to the trading captains to assist him with firearms and men. Thirty American and English seamen joined the warriors of Mbua in attacks on enemy towns, including Tavera, north of where their vessels lay. In one of the raids, the chief officer of an American ship commanded a launch in which he mounted a cannon, while the rest of the men carried guns. The warriors of Tavera fled before cannon and gunshot, leaving their old men, women, and children hiding at the water's edge.

But they were soon discoverd by their enemies, and the victory secured by the traders' guns became a slaughter. When the massacre ended, and the bodies were dismembered for cooking, the trees of Tavera were hung with human limbs, waiting to be roasted in the victory feast. One sailor, who was offered a human leg for his part in the battle, was so unnerved by the grisly aftermath that he refused to break fast for five days. Lockerby, who also participated in the battle, described the method of cooking human flesh after the body was dissected, although he says sometimes a whole body was roasted on hot stones, covered with leaves and dirt. Generally, individual limbs were wrapped in green leaves and boiled on the fire, seasoned with tara root.

Although the chief at Mbua, with the help of the trading crews, secured a tentative truce with his enemies by the end of 1808, the situation on Sandalwood Island was permanently altered. And the new destructive force of firearms, introduced in the civil wars, was fed from a fresh source: the beachcombers on the neighboring island of Viti Levu. Viti Levu is the largest of the Fiji Islands; although twice the size of Vanua Levu, having no sandalwood, it did not share in the wealth brought to her neighbor by the traders from America and New South Wales. Several of the chiefs of the towns on the southeastern tip of Viti Levu had joined in the demands for distribution of the treasury accumulated at Sandalwood Bay, and had taken part in the civil wars. Like the unsuccessful warriors on Vanua Levu, in whose battle they joined, they had, originally, nothing with which to resist the power of firearms. But in mid-1808, just as the war began, a New England sandalwood vessel, the *Eliza* of Providence, was wrecked on an island off Viti Levu with results that subsequently changed the balance of power in Fiji.

Captain Hill Correy brought the *Eliza* to Fiji from Port Jackson and Tonga after first stopping at Buenos Aires, where he assisted the English forces in opening the River Plate, which may account for his having forty thousand Spanish dollars aboard his vessel. The *Eliza* was halfway through the Koro Sea when she struck a reef at about midnight, nine miles south of the island of Nairai. Her crew of more than a dozen men lay off the wreck through the night, and the next morning reached Nairai in the long boat. The ship's master managed to bring almost all the silver dollars away in the boat, although this specie was soon appropriated by the natives. The captain remained on the island for a week, gathering back six thousand dollars that had been scattered among the inhabitants of Nairai. Then, he and four of the survivors left for Sandalwood Bay, where they knew a Yankee vessel was loading cargo for China. The captain promised the other members of the crew stranded on the island that he would return for them within a week. "I retired to a cocoanut tree," wrote one of the sailors left behind, "and sat down under it and gave vent to a flood of tears." [17] When the captain finally returned, three of his men had been taken to the island of Mbatiki while the other five had gone to Viti Levu, where they formed the first wave of a colony of beachcombers adjacent to Sandalwood Island.

Captain Correy and his four companions returned to Nairai with two well-armed boats and extra men from the *Jenny* of Boston, anchored off Sandy Hook while her cargo was being completed. Although the captain bartered small pieces of iron and other trading goods for five days with the natives, he succeeded in getting back only nine thousand of the missing silver dollars, while a skirmish with the islanders took the lives of two Americans. The Providence sea captain departed from Sandalwood Bay in the *Jenny;* however, when the vessel reached Guam, his part in assisting the British in the battle of the River Plate was disclosed to the Spanish and he was detained and his silver dollars taken from him. Captain Correy, then taking command of a Spanish vessel operating out of Guam, was again shipwrecked in the Pacific. But this time he was cast ashore on a lonely island, where he died.

Five of the survivors from the *Eliza* were taken to Viti Levu, where they became beachcombers; three other members of the crew remained for about six months at Mbatiki, an island close to the site of their shipwreck. Keeping track of the time by tying one knot in a spear of grass for each weekday and two knots for each Sunday, the sailors on Mbatiki knew when it was Christmas. They celebrated the holiday by borrowing a pot from the chief, stealing one of his fowl, and cooking it with herbs. "Thus we had our feast," recorded one of them," and felt as well, perhaps, as many would on the best dainties in America." [18] The three seamen finally succeeded in getting a canoe in which they reached Sandalwood Bay, where a vessel was loading cargo. She was a brig out of Port Jackson whose chief officer, a native of Rhode Island, made places aboard for the survivors of the Providence ship. But before the brig sailed, two of the men returned to Nairai to retrieve some of the Spanish dollars. They bartered back a large sum in silver specie, although one of the men paid for the dollars with his life in a battle with the natives.

The story of forty thousand silver dollars on Nairai spread among the sailors on other islands of Fiji and across the water to Tonga. At least two dozen castaways, deserters, and discharged seamen eventually made their way to the leeward islands of the Koro Sea in the neighborhood of Nairai, finally settling at the town of Mbau on Viti Levu under the leadership of Charles Savage, a survivor of the *Eliza.* Savage was one of the sealers at Bass Strait, in New South Wales, who participated in 1804 in

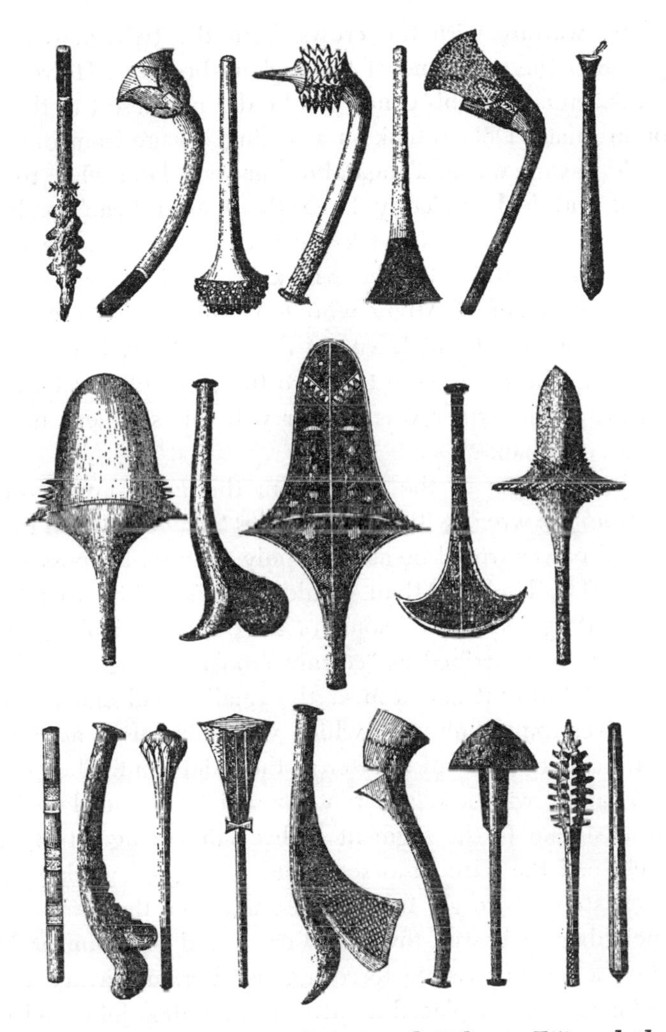

Fijian war clubs. From Williams and Calvert, *Fiji and the Fijians* (London, 1859).

the long warfare with the crews from the two New England ships under the command of the Delano brothers. However, unlike a dozen or so of his comrades, he did not desert to the vessel Captain Amasa Delano took on a sealing voyage from Bass Strait to Chile. Savage was at Tongatabu four years later when the *Eliza* arrived, and had evidently been there as a beachcomber for some time, for he could speak the native language. He was living alone at Nairai after the wreck of the *Eliza* when he was seen by the chief of Mbau who took him to his town at the southeastern end of Viti Levu. At the same time, four other survivors from the *Eliza* were taken to the town of Verata, also on Viti Levu, whose ruler was at war with his southern neighbor, the chief of Mbau.

Although none of the crew from the *Eliza* apparently got away from the wreck with guns, Charles Savage realized that survival and power would be assured only through his possession of firearms. The king of Mbau would not allow him to return to Nairai, but agreed to send some of his people to look for objects which Savage described as "certain crooked things, which were wooden at the butt and iron at the smaller end and hollow."[19] The natives found only one, which was being used as the ornamental projecting end of a rafter in the chief's hut. They brought it back, along with a keg of powder which he had described to them as similar to the pigment of his hair. Savage stripped the gun, cleaned the parts, and soon had it in good working order. His next step was to get the four seamen from the *Eliza* to leave the neighboring hostile town of Verata and join him at Mbau. Leading a reconnaissance force against Verata, Savage did not leave his canoe, but placed a letter in a bamboo joint and called to his comrades to come and fetch it from the water. One account says the letter was stuck in a gourd tied to a stick; at any rate, its message, according to legend, read: "Come to the place where I am living at Bau; it is a good place, and he is also a good chief whom I am living with."[20] The four sailors came to Mbau.

Charles Savage was, originally, the only one of the seamen on Viti Levu with a musket. His effective use of it in battle raised him to a position second only to the king of Mbau and secured him two wives of the highest rank. Designated Koroi Na Vunivalu, he was treated with the dignity of a chief, lived apart from the sailors, and maintained his individuality by always dressing in Western clothes. But, in time, other beachcombers obtained guns from the traders on Sandalwood Island, or already had them when they reached Viti Levu. "Some of our men," wrote a New England survivor from the *Eliza* who did not join Savage's colony at Mbau, "were so unwise, as to go with the natives into their battles with muskets, and kill many of the opposite party, who had never injured them, and pleased their employers much." [21] The Fijians generally treated the beachcombers well, tolerating the behavior that had led them to desertion and alienation from their own kind, because of the enormous power of their firearms. But except for Savage, whose death the people of Mbau lamented and revenged, the castaway sailors and deserters were disliked. On one occasion, when Savage was away, they dishonored a native feast and three of them were clubbed to death.

The greatest danger to the beachcombers' lives and property, however, came from among their own comrades. One of their rank, who spent three years at Mbau, told William Mariner, a sailor who passed the same length of time on Tonga: "he was heartily glad to come away, because he was afraid to live on the same island with his companions, lest he should be killed in some quarrell." [22] There were several dozen of them living at Mbau after 1809, more or less under the authority of Savage. Whenever they needed provisions—particularly liquor and tobacco—they went in canoes to Vanua Levu and worked for the American and Port Jackson traders as interpreters and boatmen. By this time, the forest behind Sandalwood Bay had been depleted, and the trade had moved northeast along the coast to Wailea Bay. The power of the friendly ruler of Mbua Bay, Tui

Na Mbouwalu, had waned with his vanishing forests and the spread of civil war; his rival at Mbau, with his band of beachcombers, was in the ascendant. The Yankee traders at Wailea kept close to their ships for protection, making their headquarters on Brown's Island, and relying on the beachcombers to work the boats carrying the sandalwood from the shore to the ship. The captains paid the beachcombers with liquor and tobacco, and with beads, mirrors, cutlery, and ironware for their own, private barter with the natives.

Sometimes, when the islanders were slow in bringing the wood down from the hills, the masters of China-bound vessels hired the beachcombers to gather *bêche-de-mer* from the coral reefs of Viti Levu. This "marine worm," as one Yankee sealing and sandalwood captain called it, was considered a great delicacy by the Chinese when made into a gelatinous soup. Varying in length from six to fifteen inches, with smooth or prickly skin, the "sea cucumber" comes in a range of colors—black, brown, yellow, and white. The brown and black brought the highest price; the white variety was not considered worth the expense of preparing, at least in the trade before the War of 1812. The men collected the trepangs from the shallow water, carrying them to a special boat covered by an awning to prevent them from melting in the sun. They were boiled on shore in a cauldron of brine, dried on a flake, and cured by the fire or sun. They were packed, for market, in baskets and mats and stowed where there was the least chance of their getting wet.

An unsuccessful expedition for *bêche-de-mer* brought Oliver Slater, the survivor from the *Argo,* back to Vanua Levu three years after he had guided the pioneering sandalwood vessel to Mbua Bay in 1801. Although he had revealed the secret of Sandalwood Island to the master of the *Fair American* in Manila, and later spread the news among the captains at Port Jackson, he did not sail in 1804 on the latter vessel, the first ship flying the Stars and Stripes to reach Canton from Fiji. Instead, he joined "in a speculative voyage in a small schooner to Wreck

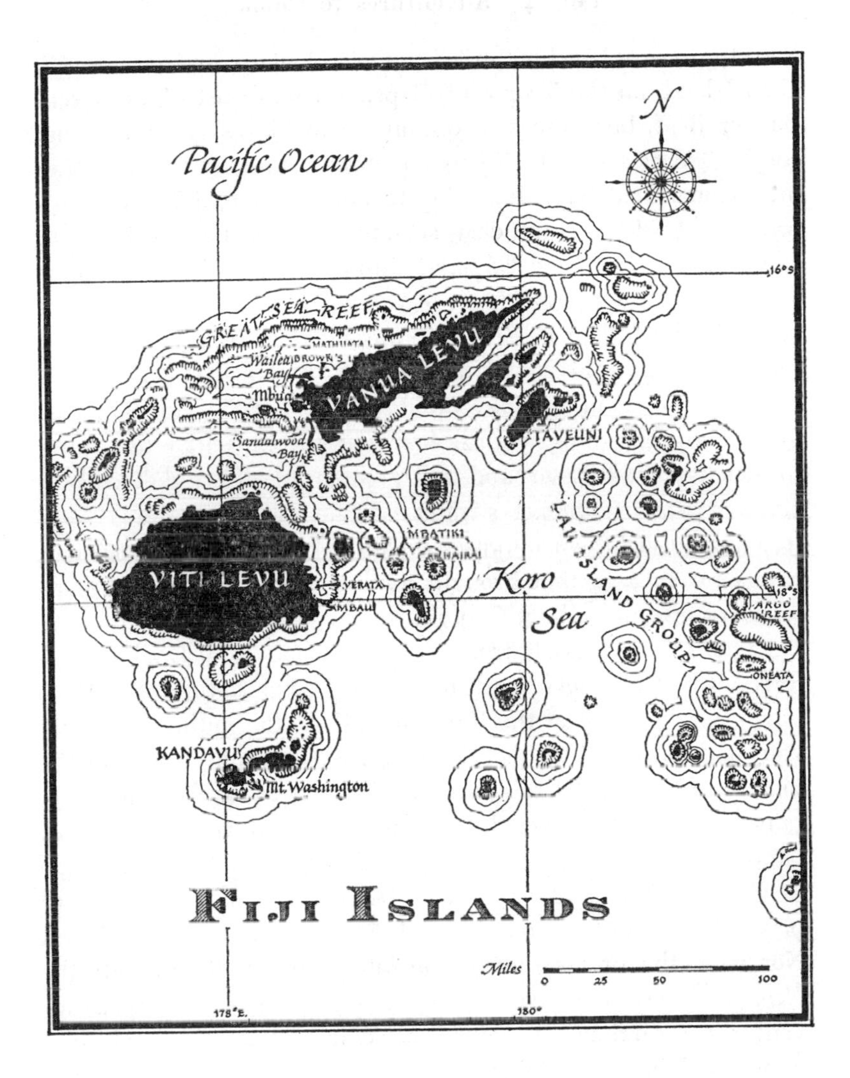

N
Pacific Ocean
16°S
GREAT SEA REEF
MATHUATA I.
Wailea Bay
BROWN'S I.
Mbua
VANUA LEVU
Sandalwood Bay
TAVEUNI
LAU ISLAND GROUP
MBATIKI
NAIRAI
VITI LEVU
VERATA
MBAU
Koro Sea
18°S
ARGO REEF
ONEATA
KANDAVU
Mt. Washington
FIJI ISLANDS
Miles
0 25 50 100
178°E.
180°

Reef to procure beechley mar."[23] The colonial vessel cleared for Cato Island, on the Tropic of Capricorn southeast of the Great Barrier Reef, but failing to obtain a suitable cargo of trepang, they sailed eastward to Fiji where Slater directed the schooner into Sandalwood Bay. Returning to Port Jackson, Slater then offered to guide a Nantucket sealing captain, Peter Chase, to Vanua Levu. The New England ship's master had reached Port Jackson in the *Criterion* from a losing voyage to the Crozet Islands, in the Indian Ocean, and was looking for a better cargo for Canton than his small lading of seal skins. The *Criterion,* which anchored in Sandalwood Bay in mid-1805, with Slater as guide and interpreter, was the first vessel from the United States to reach Vanua Levu and carry a cargo of sandalwood to China.[24] The Nantucket sealing captain bartered trinkets and iron valued at fifteen hundred dollars with the friendly ruler at Mbua for a cargo that brought almost eighty thousand dollars' worth of teas and silks at Canton.

A half-dozen vessels from New York and New England followed the *Criterion's* lead to Vanua Levu before mid-1808, when the depletion of the forests of Mbua, the outbreak of civil war, and the wreck of the *Eliza* signaled a turning point in the history of the Fiji Islands. Another half dozen Yankee ships obtained cargoes from the hills along the northwestern coast of Sandalwood Island between 1808 and 1812, despite the increase in violence and danger reflecting the change in the balance of power between Mbua on Vanua Levu and Mbau on Viti Levu. Nor were the profits during the latter period diminished: the *Hunter* of Boston, which completed one of the last American adventures in sandalwood before the War of 1812, bartered eight hundred dollars in trinkets for a cargo which realized eighty thousand dollars in trade in China. It was the outbreak of war between the United States and England that drove the Yankee traders from the waters between New South Wales and Fiji and made a run through the China Sea to Canton almost impossible.

But the trade, which now fell entirely to the rivals from Port Jackson, and a few ships from Calcutta, came to a violent end in 1814, after two massacres that took the lives of most of the American and European beachcombers.

An East Indiaman, the *Hunter* of Calcutta, anchored in Wailea Bay in the spring of 1813. Her master, a trader who had participated earlier in the civil wars in the sandalwood country, now led twenty armed men, with a cannon mounted in one of the boats, against the enemies of the ruler of Wailea. But despite the great destruction accomplished by the crew from the *Hunter*, the ruler was reluctant to fulfill his end of the bargain, and very little sandalwood was carried from the hills to the ship anchored in the bay. The trading captain, who had most of the beachcombers from Mbau, including Charles Savage, working for him, sent them and some of his own crew on an expedition against the chief of Wailea. The party was ambushed and destroyed except for two men who escaped to the ship and six others who took refuge on a large rock which they defended with their rifles. Among the six were Charles Savage and Peter Dillon, a former beachcomber at Mbau who had returned to the islands as third officer on the East Indiaman.

Savage and one of the beachcombers finally left the refuge, intending to intercede with the chief whose men were swirling about the rock. Savage was seized and held, face down, in a well of fresh water until he drowned; his companion, also a survivor from the *Eliza,* was clubbed to death. The ruler of Wailea allowed one of the remaining men on the rock, who was wounded, to return to the ship, to tell the captain to free the natives he held as hostages. The chief then sent the high priest to the rock to persuade the men to come down; but he was immediately seized by Peter Dillon. He and his two companions placed the muzzles of their guns at the priest's head and forced their way between the rock and the water through hundreds of natives. As they passed, they saw the bodies of their slain comrades, including that of Charles Savage, prepared for roasting. Dillion and the few surviving beachcombers, with their Fijian wives, sailed from Wailea Bay in the East Indiaman.

Peter Dillon eventually became master of his own ship, trading among the islands of the South Pacific. On one of his voyages, more than a dozen years after the massacre at Wailea, he anchored off the tiny island of Tikopia, in the Santa Cruz group. It was on this island, in 1813, that the East Indiaman landed two of the beachcombers, one of whom had participated with Dillon in the successful retreat from the rock with the high priest as hostage. Both men, whom Dillon had also known when he was, himself, a beachcomber on Viti Levu, were alive and well; they had been treated with great kindness by the natives. Captain Dillon was surprised to see that they had some silver objects of European make—a sword guard, a fork, and knives—as well as cups and bottles. When they told him they came from the neighboring island of Vanikoro, where there still remained other objects from two vessels wrecked there long ago, Dillon concluded they belonged to the ships in the expedition of La Pérouse, which had left New South Wales in 1788 and had never been heard of again. The next year, in 1827, Dillon led a search from Calcutta to Vanikoro, whose coral reefs yielded many more relics from the ill-fated French voyage of discovery. For this service, the former beachcomber of Mbau was made an officer of the *Légion d'honneur*.

Although the massacre at Wailea was described in the Port Jackson newspapers, a sandalwood expedition set out for that dangerous bay in mid-1814. The adventure was led by a veteran trader whose brig carried Oliver Slater as chief officer. The colonial vessel anchored north of Sandalwood Bay, in the domain of the ruler whose now declining town had reaped the first riches of the sandalwood trade. Oliver Slater and three sailors, two of them also Americans, went northeast along the coast in a small boat to Wailea Bay to determine the possibility of communication and trade with the natives. The four men were killed as soon as they reached the town of Wailea, which Peter Dillon described as "situated on the verdant banks of a beautiful stream." [25] The brig returned to Port Jackson with a small cargo —the final adventure in sandalwood in the period that closed with the War of 1812. The sandalwood trade, which began a dozen years earlier when Oliver Slater was found living on an island in the Koro Sea, ended with his death on the northern shore of Vanua Levu.

10

Polynesia

A year after the last Yankee trading vessel departed from Vanua Levu, an American naval officer proposed a sandalwood adventure at the Marquesas Islands. Captain David Porter made his suggestion in the fall of 1813 from a haven at Nuku Hiva, several thousand miles eastward across the Pacific from Fiji. He reached Nuku Hiva, one of the largest of the Marquesas Islands, from a cruise in the South Atlantic where he captured the first British sloop in the War of 1812, and along the west coast of South America where he seized a number of English whaling ships. Now resting at Nuku Hiva, Captain Porter estimated a full cargo of sandalwood for Canton could be cut in the hills and carried to the ship for a barter of ten whale teeth. "I have seen them," he wrote of the natives, "by fits laugh and cry for joy, at the possession of one of these darling treasures." [1] But the sandalwood race at the Marquesas did not begin until 1815, when several vessels out of Port Jackson arrived at the islands on the eastern fringe of Polynesia and commenced to barter there for this valuable China-trading item.

There was, however, a lone attempt made by an American vessel to obtain a cargo of sandalwood at the Marquesas in the period that ended with the War of 1812. The vessel, the *Albatross,* was one of three Boston ships trading to China with cargoes that included sandalwood from Hawaii and seal skins from the coast of California. For her expected sandalwood adventure at the Marquesas, she was chartered at Honolulu by Wilson Hunt, an agent for John Astor. Arriving at Nuku Hiva in November of 1813, he learned from Captain Porter that a British squadron was sailing toward the Northwest Coast with the colony at Astoria one of their objectives; the *Albatross* was ordered immediately back to Hawaii. Captain Porter lingered for five months at Nuku Hiva, interfering in the native wars and claiming the island for the United States. He sailed for South America early in 1814 and reached the coast of Chile, where he was joined in the harbor of Valparaíso by two English warships. The American commander hoped to engage the rival warships separately, but after evading this stratagem for a number of weeks, the British vessels entered the harbor and captured the Yankee frigate.

Nuku Hiva had actually been claimed for the United States several decades earlier, when two Boston shipmasters trading to China visited the island in 1791 and 1792. In the latter year, Captain Josiah Roberts brought the *Jefferson* to the Marquesas from the coast of Chile, where he led one of the first two American sealing adventures in the Pacific and the initial hunt on the islands of San Félix and San Ambrosio. Captain Roberts rendezvoused three months at Tahuata, his crew feasting on hogs and building a small schooner. Exploring the islands north of his anchorage, the sealing captain believed they were not included in the Marquesas group discovered by Alvara de Mendãna in 1595 and re-discovered by Captain Cook a hundred and eighty years later. To the island of Nuku Hiva, he gave the name Washington, as it was "the parent of all this cluster of Islands." [2] He did not know that another New England China-trader, Captain Joseph Ingraham, had preceded him to the northern Marquesas.

Captain Ingraham, sailing the *Hope* through the islands in April of 1791, concluded they had never been seen before by "civilized" man and took possession of them for his native country. Anchoring off Nuku Hiva, he claimed the island for the United States: "On which we all gave three cheers and confirmed the name of WASHINGTON'S *island.*" [3]

When Captain Edmund Fanning brought his sealing vessel *Betsey* to the Marquesas in 1798, he considered them and the "Washington Group" two separate geographic areas. Captain Fanning was on his way to China with a large cargo of seal skins obtained earlier in the year at Más Afuera, which he rediscovered for the Yankee hunters. Lying off the island of Tahuata, he was surprised to see a white man approaching the vessel in a canoe; it was an Englishman, William Cook, who paddled out to warn that the natives planned to attack the New York brig and massacre her crew. Cook had arrived at the Marquesas in the missionary ship *Duff*, some of whose female passengers reached Vanua Levu from Tahiti and were admired by the chief of Wailea as possible barter for sandalwood. With the missionary aboard, the vessel drifted among the islands of the Washington Group until the natives again plotted to capture her at a place Captain Fanning named Escape Bay. However, at Nuku Hiva, the sealing captain was hospitably received by the king and queen; here, he noted, "all the ladies were besmeared with a mixture of cocoa oil and perfume of sandalwood." [4] This custom originally led another group of Polynesians, the Tongans, to Fiji for sandalwood.

Like his predecessors at the Marquesas, who gave New England names to almost all the islands and islets in the Washington Group, Captain Fanning named a number of uncharted islands as well as various bays and promontories. On the last lap of her passage to China, the *Betsey* touched at several coral atolls about fifteen hundred miles northeast of the Marquesas which Captain Fanning failed to locate on any of his charts. The sealers went ashore on one of them, which was named Fanning Island in honor of its discoverer, and found a grove of coconut palms where the fruit lay three feet deep on the ground. Forming a chain between the grove and the shore, the crew swiftly filled a boatload from the fresh, top layer.

Although Fanning Island and its neighbor, Washington Island, still retain the names given at this time, most of the designations made by the sealing and sandalwood captains have disappeared. Washington was the name most often used by the newly independent American mariners who sailed, for the first time in their national ships, east of Capetown and west of the Horn. But this designation, which once held meaning and memory for Yankee sealers and sandalwood traders—from Port Washington among the snows of Kerguelen to Mount Washington in the humid Koro Sea—has largely vanished from the geography of the southern oceans, along with "Dutch Church" on Más Afuera, "Sandy Hook" on Vanua Levu, and another "Fanning Island" in the Crozets.

"The Pacific Ocean," wrote the supercargo of the *Neptune*, bound from Más Afuera to Hawaii, "is fully entitled to its name."[5] The *Neptune*, like most of the Yankee vessels that hunted off the west and east coasts of South America, rode the southeast trades across the Pacific to the equator and the northeast trades from there to the Hawaiian Islands. They were further from their destination than their countrymen sealing in the Indian Ocean and Australasia, or trading at Fiji, who followed the track of the spice ships to Indonesia and the South China Sea. Except for a few of the pioneers, the New England and New York sealing captains who completed cargoes in the South Atlantic and the Southeastern Pacific bypassed the Marquesas to refit and provision their vessels at the Hawaiian Islands. Lying along the Tropic of Cancer, they formed the northern limits of Polynesia and were the "tropical isles" known and beloved by the Yankee sealers.

The Hawaiian Islands were then called the Sandwich Islands, the name given by Captain Cook who visited them twice on his last voyage of exploration. Cook is considered to be the discoverer of Hawaii, and it was during a skirmish on the largest of the islands, his "Owhyhee," that he was struck from behind by a native, fell face downward into the water, and was killed by blows from clubs and daggers. "Thus," lamented his successor, "fell our great and excellent Commander!" [6] The slaying of Captain Cook at Kealakekua Bay in the second month of 1779 gave the islands an evil reputation, and no British vessels touched there for almost a decade. But in 1787, Captains Nathaniel Portlock and George Dixon, who served under Cook on his last voyage, visited Hawaii on their way to the Northwest Coast. Earlier on this voyage, the two English captains stopped at the Falkland Islands, where they attempted to purchase the seal skins taken there by the ship *United States,* sailing out of Nantucket. For Portlock and Dixon were bound on a trading expedition to China and hoped to include, if possible, seal skins among their cargo for Canton.

Instead, the seal skins obtained by the Nantucket vessel at the Falklands were sold at Manhattan in 1786 and carried to Macao in the New York brig *Eleanora.* This was the first significant shipment of skins to be offered in the China market by a Yankee trader; earlier vessels from the United States carried pelts as only a minor part of their cargoes. The master of the *Eleanora,* Simon Metcalf, was also the first American sealing captain to reach the Hawaiian Islands. After disposing of his seal skins at Canton in the fall of 1788, Captain Metcalf purchased a small schooner at Macao which he named the *Fair American* and placed under the command of his eighteen-year-old son. The two vessels sailed together the following year for the Northwest Coast, but were parted by a storm off Japan. They reached the area of Vancouver Island separately, never having made contact anywhere along the mainland. The little twenty-six-ton schooner was captured by the Spanish, who at that time claimed the Northwest Territory and maintained a small outpost at Nootka Sound on Vancouver Island. With the *Fair American* held as a prize, the Spanish sighted and attempted to capture a brig off Nootka Sound believed to be the *Eleanora,* but she escaped. After being taken all the way to Mexico, the schooner *Fair American* was restored to the young commander who set her sails for the Hawaiian Islands.

The two Metcalfs made their ways independently to Hawaii, both anchoring off the island of Maui early in 1790, the second American vessels to reach the islands. The *Eleanora* was lying off the town of Olualu when the natives stole one of the small boats and killed a sailor who was sleeping in it. After breaking up the boat for its iron, the islanders offered the bones of the slain sailor for sale. Captain Metcalf took a terrible revenge; loading his guns with grapeshot, he fired directly into a fleet of canoes that were waiting to trade off the starboard side of his vessel. A New England sea captain, who kept a journal at Hawaii the following year, described the massacre which claimed over a hundred lives, and suggested "these islanders, as well as many others in this ocean, have abundant reason to lament they were ever discovered." [7]

Captain Metcalf did not know that shortly after the massacre at Olualu his son anchored off a town on the opposite side of Maui. The *Eleanora* lay at the larger island of Hawaii at the time young Metcalf brought the *Fair American* into Kawaihae Bay with a company of only five men. The defenseless state of the schooner and the great value to the islanders of any vessel made her the prey of one of the chiefs of Maui, who was also eager to avenge a flogging he received from the elder Metcalf. The chief carried a feathered cap when he and his people came to the *Fair American* to trade; he offered the headpiece to the young captain and when Metcalf took it in his hands, the chief seized him and threw him overboard. At the same moment, the islanders overpowered the other members of the crew and tossed them into the water where all but one were beaten to death with paddles. The lone survivor was Isaac Davis, whose battered body was thrown on the beach. In time, Davis recovered and became one of the two legacies that fell to the king of Hawaii as a result of the massacres at Maui.

The other legacy was John Young, boatswain on the *Eleanora,* then loading sandalwood at Kealakekua Bay, where Captain Cook was slain. The ruler of the island, Kamehameha, who controlled Maui as well as Hawaii and later became king of all the islands, feared that Captain Metcalf would hear about the capture of his son's vessel and turn his guns upon the town, as he did at Olualu. To prevent the chance of any news reaching the vessel, Kamehameha placed all the canoes under taboo, so that no one, including John Young who was ashore, could leave the beach; the *Eleanora* sailed without her boatswain. Captain Metcalf went on to Canton and from there embarked on the unsuccessful sealing voyage that took him to Kerguelen, Cook's "Island of Desolation." Kamehameha befriended both John Young and Isaac Davis, who contributed significantly to the chief's conquest of the neighboring islands through their efficiency in the use of firearms. The former seamen were carried into battle on the shoulders of natives who set them down at strategic places from which they fired their guns; after reloading, they were again placed on the islanders' shoulders and rushed off to another area of battle. When Kamehameha conquered Oahu and moved, with Davis, to Honolulu, he made Young the governor of the island of Hawaii.

Davis and Young played an important role in Kamehameha's profitable and successful relations with the visiting shipmasters and sandalwood traders. Ever since the arrival of the first China-bound vessels, the future king encouraged communication and trade with Hawaii; it is recorded he was extremely angry with the chief of Maui over the capture of the *Fair American* and the slaughter of most of her crew. Both Kamehameha and his queen personally begged American and English seamen to settle on the islands, granting them land, houses, and wives. When Captain Amasa Delano arrived in 1806 from a losing voyage at Bass

Strait and the Southeastern Pacific, he noted the fine house and lands granted to a ship's master who he knew during the great days of sealing on Más Afuera at the turn of the century. One of the king's favorites was Oliver Holmes, who came to the islands as a young New England seaman shortly after the massacres at Maui and remained to become a chief, married a Polynesian princess, and eventually was made governor of Oahu. Holmes and another former seaman, John Wood, exerted considerable influence upon the sandalwood trade in Hawaii. The captain of a New York vessel trading to China noted that "old John Wood" was responsible for almost all the king's decisions as to whom, and under what conditions, sandalwood contracts were granted.[8]

The seamen who settled on the islands and became agents and administrators to the king benefited in many ways from the profits in trade. "We have wasted," complained the supercargo of the *Maryland*, at Honolulu in 1806 after failing to obtain seal skins at either the South Atlantic or Pacific, "much time and money here. Our numerous visitors have proved a heavy tax in the article of gin alone, upwards of five hundred large bottles have been consumed, great part by the thirsty whites."[9] The Yankee captains came to the islands to refit and provision their vessels for the last lap of the passage to Canton. The crew of the *Betsey* of New Haven, with over a hundred thousand seal skins in her hold, sojourned two weeks off Diamond Head in 1800, painting the ship, overhauling the rigging, and mending sail. The sealing vessels took on water and huge quantities of food—hogs, fowl, potatoes, bananas, coconuts, and sugar cane—for which they bartered pieces of iron and nails. The Hawaiians displayed the same avid interest in iron shown everywhere in Polynesia and Fiji in the early stages of the Pacific trade. "The King of Owhyee looked to my occupation with a wistful eye," recorded the cooper on the first China-trading vessel to reach the island after the death of Captain Cook, "he thought me the happiest man on board, to be among such vast heaps of treasure."[10] The cooper fashioned one of the standard articles of barter: barrel and cask hoops cut into lengths of eight or nine inches with one end brought to a sharp point.

Sealers one hundred and fifty miles out at sea could see the mountains of Hawaii on a clear day. It was a memorable sight for those who made the islands their first landfall from the hunting grounds of the Southeastern Pacific. Nor did the islands or the islanders, especially the women, fail to fulfill the mariners' expectations. "Not much work done this afternoon," noted a New England seaman whose vessel was loading sandalwood at Oahu, "being girls on board—going from ship to ship."[11] When it came time to quit the islands, many among the sealing crews had to be dragged or carried aboard by their comrades or the ship's master was forced to pay Kamehameha and his chiefs rewards in iron, cloth, and tobacco for the return of runaway sailors. For no matter how long the vessels tarried at Hawaii—the *Huron* was there two months on her way to Canton from the seal islands of Santa Maria and Mocha, while the *Neptune,* also out of New Haven, remained only three weeks on her passage from Más Afuera—it was never time enough for the ship's company. But six days out, bound for China, the physician on the *Betsey,* who headed her sealing gang for two lonely years at Más Afuera, recorded another side of the visit: "Five with the veneral disorder."[12] A week later, the number was placed at seven.

The visiting seamen often went to Kealakekua Bay to stand on the spot where Captain Cook was slain. His burial place is described by a member of a Boston sealing and trading expedition as "a beautiful, sequestered spot, of a circular form, surrounded with banana and cocoa-nut trees, the grave occupying the center of the circle."[13] The man credited with striking down Captain Cook traded with the sealing vessels but never went aboard, returning alone to the shore. The supercargo of the *Neptune,* arriving at Hawaii from a winter's hunt on the wind-swept island of Más Afuera, went swimming with the natives who "laughed very heartily at seeing my white shoulders among their dark ones."[14] He also tells of having a double canoe tattooed on his leg and how his men were cheated by the islanders who sold them straw mats which proved to be only half finished when unrolled on shipboard.

The celebration of the Fourth of July by American seamen at Hawaii was unique among the islands of the Pacific. The festivities began at noon when the vessels, dressed overhaul, fired their first rounds in salute; improvised bands played "Hail Columbia" during the afternoon, between rounds of drinks on shipboard and shore, and a final round of shots fired in salute at sunset. The supercargo of the *Maryland* described the Fourth of July 1806, when Kamehameha and the royal family came aboard his ship and "celebrated the day in streams of gin." He adds: "One half of our crew were rioting on shore, and could with great difficulty be got off again."[15] Eight years later, midway in the War of 1812, the crews from a number of Yankee ships celebrated the anniversity of their nation's independence on Kaui with thirteen toasts that honored the king of the island, commerce, and "The Ladies of the Sandwich Islands, while embracing their charms, let us not forget the Yankee fair ones at home."[16] The toasts were made possible through the contribution of a quantity of Madeira by Captain Jonathan Winship, who formed a partnership at Honolulu with Captains Nathan Winship and William Davis to revive the American trade in sandalwood between Hawaii and Canton.

Known as the "Lords of the Pacific," the three Boston shipmasters operated along the coast of California a number of years before settling at Hawaii. Jonathan Winship first arrived in California in 1804 as mate on his family's ship *O'Cain;* he returned in 1806 as master of the vessel with his brother, Nathan, first mate; Nathan Winship next appeared on the coast in 1809 in command of the *Albatross;* the third partner, and ship, in the sandalwood trade, William Davis of the *Isabella,* met his future associates while sealing off San Francisco in 1810. The Winships were originally drawn to California in pursuit of the sea otter, the prey of the American China-traders on the Northwest Coast. Taking aboard more than one hundred Kodiak Indians at a Russian settlement in Alaska, as well as their food supply of "15,400 dried fish and 1000 pounds of whale flesh," they set out on a voyage in mid-1806 that brought the *O'Cain* to the islands off Vizcaíno Bay, about four hundred miles south of San Diego.[17] The vessel traded along the mainland, at the neighboring mission towns, while the Kodiaks hunted in their leather canoes for sea otter, and a small party of American sailors and natives of Hawaii were left on the island of Cedros to kill seals.

Hawaiian seamen were often included among the ship's company of sealing vessels after the first Yankee hunters reached the islands from Más Afuera in 1798. They were particularly active among the gangs that hunted the off-shore islands of Chile and Peru for long periods of time, such as the voyages of the Delano brothers, and were among the best fighters in the Delanos' battles with the gangs from New South Wales for control of the seal islands in Bass Strait. The year after the Winships brought their Hawaiian hunters to Lower California, the veteran sealing captain Caleb Brintnall hired a number of the islanders for an expedition in his ship *Triumph,* including a twelve-year-old boy called Henry Obookiah. One of the Yankee seamen on the voyage, recently graduated from Yale, taught the boy to speak the English language. Obookiah remained on the ship after the skins were sold at Canton, returning to New England with Captain Brintnall. The young Hawaiian lived with the ship's master in his house at New Haven, where he made friends among the students at Yale. One of them, Edwin Dwight, wrote a memoir of Henry Obookiah after the Hawaiian's death in Connecticut in 1817.[18]

Although seal skins were not the principal objective of the voyage of the *O'Cain* to Lower California in 1806, the vessel returned the following year and again left a gang of hunters on the island of Cedros. The island was visited the next season by the *Dromo* of Boston, which had been trading for a number of years off the west coast of South America. One of her seamen said twenty thousand seals lined the rocky beach at Cedros when they arrived, although most of them escaped to the water when forty men from the ship went ashore to hunt. The *Dromo* lay off the "wild and inhospitable" island for a week, while her crew killed, dried, and stacked three thousand skins for the Canton market. The Yankee ships that hunted the seal and the sea otter along the California coast also traded for skins at the Spanish settlements. The trade was eagerly sought by the mission fathers who often lived in extreme isolation among the Indians; a New York sealing and trading captain comments on one such transaction: "rest assur'd that I have shav'd the Padres well." [19] Trading, and hunting within ninety miles of the shore, was illegal, and occasionally the Spanish made an effort to enforce the ban which extended to all foreign vessels. Captain George Eyres of Boston was captured off Santa Barbara in 1813 in his ship *Mercury*, and the crew confined to the local presidio; the Captain was allowed a dollar a day for support, his men only twenty cents apiece. The captain's Hawaiian "wife," who bore him a child a few days before the vessel was captured, remained in California, became a Catholic, and relinquished her Polynesian name for that of María Antonia de la Ascension.

The principal sealing expeditions along the California coast were concentrated on the Farallone Islands, about eighty miles out to sea from the Bay of San Francisco. These bleak islands were first explored by the *O'Cain* in 1807, when it was discovered they were a haven for the fur and hair seal. The latter vessel returned to the Farallones in mid-1810, when she was joined by the *Albatross* and the *Isabella*. The Lords of the Pacific maintained Polynesian sealing gangs on the Farallones until early in 1812; it is estimated the Hawaiian hunters, under Yankee leaders, obtained about one hundred and fifty thousand seal skins for the Canton market. But late in 1811, the three New England shipmasters transferred their main activities from California to the island of Oahu. There, they joined with the master of another Boston vessel, the *Otter,* to revive the American trade in sandalwood between Hawaii and China initiated two decades earlier by Simon Metcalf in the *Eleanora.*

Captain Metcalf was loading a cargo of sandalwood at Kealakekua Bay on the island of Hawaii at the time his son's vessel was captured off Maui early in 1790. When Kamehameha prevented the news of the massacre from reaching the ship by imposing a taboo upon the native boats, the New York sealing captain departed with an incomplete cargo even though he could see the canoes, which "covered the shore for several miles," still laden with sandalwood.[20] The following year, Captain John Kendrick of Boston returned to Hawaii, where he is credited with acquiring a shipment of sandalwood which was sold in China. Kendrick was the master of the sloop *Washington,* tender to the *Columbia* whose voyage brought the first Americans to the Northwest Coast and Hawaii. Captain Kendrick separated from the commander of the expedition and never brought the sloop, which he altered to a brig, back to New England. He was killed at Honolulu when one of the guns misfired during a celebration in the harbor.

No further attempts were made by Americans to obtain sandalwood at the islands for twenty years. The future sealing captain Amasa Delano, at Canton when the first shipment reached there from Hawaii, says Captain Metcalf's wood was of a spurious type and judged valueless by the merchants. At any rate, Kamehameha was telling visiting shipmasters in the first years of the nineteenth century of his own intention to open a trade in sandalwood; and in 1807, a Boston mercantile house suggested that their agent in China consider a "trade in sandalwood from Canton to the islands, as long as vessels and crews will hold together." [21] It was late in 1811 before the Yankee trade in sandalwood at Hawaii was re-established. At this time, the Lords of the Pacific arrived from California with about seventy-five thousand seal skins, an insufficient cargo to provide trade for three vessels at the China market. But their joint cargo was greatly enhanced over the next two months by the addition of a supply of sandalwood acquired through barter with Kamehameha and the lesser chiefs.

After disposing of their ladings at Canton, the three New England traders settled on the island of Oahu, where they signed a contract with the king which promised them a ten-year monopoly of the sandalwood trade and assured Kamehameha one-quarter of the net sales at Canton. The king guaranteed to supply the best wood from all the islands under his control, to secure the co-operation of the local chiefs, and to allow the native gangs to be supervised by a member of the crew from each of the Boston ships. The sandalwood trees in Hawaii belonged to the reigning chief, just as they did at Vanua Levu in Fiji, and Kamehameha, under the guidance of his ex-sailor advisers, attempted to protect the trade for his sons by allowing only the mature trees to be cut.

Although the three Yankee captains resented the interference of the king's advisers, the terms of the contract were mutually honored for about one year. During this time, the sandalwood traders kept two of their vessels at the island of Oahu; the third was sent back to California to get the Polynesian gang off the Farallones and to search for new seal hunting grounds. A sufficient supply of wood was obtained by the fall of 1812 to load the two ships, which reached Canton early in 1813 where their commanders learned of the War of 1812. Hurrying back to the islands without obtaining the full proceeds from the trade in sandalwood, the Lords of the Pacific made the only voyage under the terms of their contract with the king, who received an incomplete shipment that included nankeens, shoes, hats, two beds, and a sedan chair. And while Kamehameha eventually obtained his full share in goods and money, delivered by another ship dispatched from Canton, his attitude toward the traders was altered by the changing events of the war and by the influence of his principal administrators, who, except for the Yankee Oliver Holmes, were Englishmen; although both Isaac Davis and John Young had arrived at the islands on American vessels.

Oliver Holmes, the governor of the island of Oahu, bore the

brunt of the traders' frustrations over the disintegration of their sandalwood monopoly and the rumors of a British blockade of American ships at Canton. They disputed the governor's authority with threats, blows, and even attempted to shoot him. Holmes had to use all his power to prevent the islanders from killing the Lords of the Pacific; one of whom, Captain William Davis, later became the son-in-law to the governor, marrying his American-Polynesian daughter, Hannah Holmes. The Yankee colony at Oahu was continually increased by new arrivals from the Northwest Coast, where more than a dozen American ships were trading when war was declared on England by the United States. A huge cargo of skins from some of these ships was carried from Oahu to Canton in the autumn of 1813 by the schooner *Tamaahmaah,* sailing from Boston under letters of marque and reprisals to warn vessels in the North Pacific of the war. A similar expedition by an armed merchantman was proposed by John Astor to the pioneering sealing captain Daniel Greene of New Haven. Answering Astor's letter requesting him to locate "good Sealmen" for the privateering and trading voyage, Captain Greene asked for five thousand dollars if he reached the Pacific, twenty-five hundred if not, and one-half of the prize money and net proceeds from the sale of the skins at Canton for the officers and crew, exclusive of his own share.

Captain Greene's privateering voyage was never undertaken, although the *Tamaahmaah* successfully disposposed of its cargo of skins at Canton and returned safely home to the United States. The American victories in the Pacific in the first year of the war, which brought Captain Porter's frigate to a well-earned rest at the Marquesas in the fall of 1813, were never again duplicated. Two British sloops of war soon appeared off the island of Hawaii, and in January of the next year, 1814, the Yankees retreated to the village of Waimea on Kauai, the most western of the islands. Kamehameha responded to the superior fighting power of the English ships by accusing the New Englanders of fleeing from them "as the smoke of Mona-Rowa is driven by the wind."[22] However, he promised to protect their lives and property if they would move to the island of Hawaii; but the presence there of the British warships kept the Yankees on the distant island of Kauai, which was still semi-independent of King Kamehameha. The visitors found the natives at Kauai hostile, extorting a huge barter for food and the labor to build several houses near the shore where the Americans "erect a flag staff and display the flag."[23] There was little to occupy the seamen at the village of Waimea in 1814 and 1815; they worked on the vessels in the bay, aired the skins, and visited among themselves.

The Lords of the Pacific signed a sandalwood contract with the king at Kauai similar to the one they had held earlier with Kamehameha, and some wood began to arrive from the hills about the middle of 1814. But Kamehameha, dissatisfied with the tribute he received from the king at Kauai, induced the British ships to go to Waimea, where they captured one of the Yankee vessels that was lying outside the bay. The Americans, on the other hand, were reluctant to support the king of Kauai in his defiance of Kamehameha, as they had originally promised, and the barter in sandalwood ceased entirely. After the natives attempted to burn the houses where the skins and wood were stored, the three sandalwood trading captains informed the king they intended to destroy the town by gunfire unless he continued the terms of their contract. Although the king refused, and all the the Americans took refuge on shipboard, they did not carry out their threat. In fact, Captain Davis continued to reside at Hawaii, known among the islanders as "Iliahi"; but the Winship brothers retired from the sea to a suburb of Boston, where they cultivated a famous garden.

The Yankee vessels that hunted the seal islands of the Southeastern Pacific sailed the last lap of the voyage to China after a visit at Hawaii ranging from two weeks to two months. They departed with a large quantity of hogs; the crew of the *Neptune* had to knock out the teeth of all their hogs a month after leaving the islands since they were destroying the decks by rooting with their snouts. As long as the hogs could be kept alive on shipboard, their meat was eaten fresh roasted, but on the homeward journey it was served as salt pork. The passage from the islands of Polynesia to Canton was a quiet one: "Carpenter had a little dinner," noted the physician on a New Haven sealing vessel a week out of Honolulu; ten days later he recorded "All on board in good spirits keeping Independence Day and drinking to absent friends." When they reached the warm Philippine Sea: "A number went swimming." [24] The *Betsey* of New York, one of the few sealing vessels to refresh at the Marquesas, celebrated the Fourth of July in the Philippine Sea: "Butchered our last Nuggoheeva hog," wrote her captain, "and with a full allowance of fresh pork, yams, sweet potatoes, cocoa-nuts, plum pudding, and the like savory dishes, managed matters to have a pretty jovial time of it, topping all off with a moderate glass to prevent our choking." [25] Their hogs were taken aboard at Nuku Hiva, the Yankees' "Washington Island."

The sealing vessels made a brief stop on the passage between Hawaii and Canton at the island of Tinian in the Mariana Islands. They took on wood, water, and fruit and traded with the Spaniards for tobacco. The supercargo on a New England vessel at Tinian in 1798 bartered for "some Manilla cigars of an uncouth length, but the pleasantest I ever smoked." [26] The sealers who reached Tinian that year from Polynesia found the shore littered with broken chinaware, part of the cargo from a ship that was wrecked on her voyage from Canton to the west coast of South America. The ships sailed across the Philippine Sea from Tinian, passed through the Bashi Channel separating Luzon and Formosa, and entered the South China Sea. With the mainland of Asia finally before them, they made for the Portuguese settlement of Macao at the mouth of the river that leads to Canton.

11

Canton

The Yankee sealing vessels dropped anchor outside Macao in the wide estuary of the Pearl River, a branch of the Si-kiang which flows westward a thousand miles beyond Canton. The little peninsula of Macao and the city of Canton, eighty miles upriver, were the only ports in China opened to European and American traders. The Portuguese, the first Westerners to sail to China by way of the Cape of Good Hope, had held Macao since the middle of the sixteenth century; the English established an effective trade with China at the end of the seventeenth century and were confined with other Europeans to a small area of Canton. England's commerce with China was the monopoly of the East India Company, and no vessels from her American colonies shared in the trade. But in the fall of 1784, less than a year after peace was concluded between the former colonies and mother country, the pioneering American ship *Empress of China* reached Macao from New York. Sailing the eastern passage, her master wrote they "had the honor of hoisting the first Continantal Flagg Ever Seen or maid Euse of in those

Seas." [1] The New York ship saluted the inhabitants of Macao with seven guns as she entered the estuary; the salute was honored from the fort although almost no one on the mainland of Asia knew who "Americans" were.

The Portuguese settlement at Macao provisioned the vessels with fish, fowl, and pork; good wine at seventy-five cents a bottle; and eggs and oranges at fifty cents per one hundred. Provisions and facilities at Macao were less expensive than at Canton, and many Europeans, and some Americans, lived there during the months when no business was transacted at the Chinese trading capital. "Each house has a billiard-table," noted the supercargo of the first United States ship to reach Macao, "many individuals keep pleasure boats, there is a public concert twice a week." [2] The sealing captains obtained permission from the customs officials at Macao to transact business at Canton and took aboard a licensed pilot who guided the vessel sixty miles upriver to Whampoa. This was as far into the interior of China as foreign ships were allowed. A number of costly fees were paid to the mandarins at Whampoa before the ship's master received the "chop" which enabled him to trade at Canton.

Some of the early sealing captains tried to evade the high duties imposed at Whampoa by leaving their vessels among the islands off Macao. The usual anchorage for those attempting to thwart the mandarins was Lark's Bay—sometimes called Dirty Butter Bay—about a dozen miles southwest of Macao. Captain Simon Metcalf, who carried the initial American shipment of seal skins to China in 1788, kept his brig *Eleanora* in this area while the cargo was sold at Canton. The *Eliza* of New York, the second Yankee ship to bring seal skins to China and the first to hunt at Más Afuera, lay at Lark's Bay in 1792 while her master and his agent, the future sealing captain Amasa Delano, went to Canton to ascertain the market in skins. However, the mandarins had tightened their control by this time, and the *Eliza*'s captain, William Stewart, was thrown into jail and forced to pay a heavy fine. It was a serious offense to come to Canton without first bringing the vessel to Whampoa and submitting to all the duties and charges. The attempt was more or less abandoned by sealing captains who came later, although in 1801 the master of the *Enterprise* tried to save the expense of the official duties by selling his ship at Macao and transferring a cargo of twenty-five thousand skins to another New England vessel. But an explosion occurred on the latter vessel and several men were killed; in the investigation, the *Enterprise*'s skins were discovered and her former captain had to pay double for all expenses and duties.

Aside from the likelihood of detection by the mandarins, ships lying in the vicinity of Lark's Bay, or any of the islands off Macao unprotected by the Portuguese or Chinese, were exposed to great danger from the pirates who hunted the waters of the South China Sea. While Captain Metcalf saved money by selling his skins at Canton without taking his vessel to Whampoa, it cost the lives of two of his men. The New York brig, remaining at anchor in the vicinity of Lark's Bay, was boarded by pirates, who were driven off with the loss of several members of the *Eleanora*'s crew. One sensational battle between a Yankee vessel and Malayan pirates occurred in 1809 when the Boston ship *Atahualpa* was attacked off Macao by twenty-two ladrone junks, some twice the tonnage of the Bay State vessel. The attack occurred while the New England ship was lying at the roads, waiting for a pilot to take her upriver to Whampoa. A noted pirate, Appotesi, led the assault which was witnessed by thousands of spectators who lined the shore and the hills of Macao. The *Atahualpa,* carrying three hundred thousand Spanish dollars to trade at Canton, was a tempting prize, and the battle for her possession raged for almost an hour before the Yankee ship got under the protection of the guns of the Portuguese fort.

After securing permission to go to Whampoa and taking aboard a Chinese pilot, the sealing vessels ran up the estuary to the mouth of the Pearl River. The Pearl (Ch-kiang) is a tributary of the great Si-kiang which divides about thirty miles above Canton and reaches the sea west of Macao; the Pearl runs past

Canton and sweeps into the sea at the Boca Tigre. The "Tiger's Gate" is the steep and narrow entrance to the Pearl River, which flows to Whampoa through alluvial plains; the course took two or three days. It was an anxious passage for the sealing captains, who disliked entrusting their vessels to the Chinese pilots with their reputation for running visiting ships into shoal waters. But foreigners wishing to trade at Canton were helpless before the regulations imposed through the mandarins, for the Chinese did not seek their commerce nor allow any unnecessary intercourse.

The first visitor the sealing vessel received at the anchorage at Whampoa was the "hoppo," the chief customs officer, who was also called "John Tuck." The English called him by that name because a gallows was constructed on the hoppo's boat. (Most of the designations for the Chinese officials and their regulations were of Portuguese origin; the language that served between the English-speaking seamen and the Chinese was pidgin English.) The hoppo arrived in great state and received the gifts the captain reserved for him before he performed the ceremony of measuring the vessel "which occupied at least as much time as would have taken an American surveyor to take the dimensions of twenty ships." [3] The hoppo's measurements determined the "Emperor's Duty" or customs of entrance, the primary payment for any foreign vessel to open trading negotiations. The sealing vessel *Favourite* of Nantucket, arriving at Whampoa with the cargo of skins taken at the Antipodes by the crew of the unlucky *Union,* paid almost four thousand dollars "to cumshaw to the mandarins." [4] The emperor's duty, although the largest of the fees, was merely the first of a series of commitments undertaken by a ship's master or his agent before the trading cargo of skins or sandalwood could "come ashore."

The ship's master or supercargo next engaged a "fiador," one of the hong or security merchants of Canton authorized to do business with Westerners. Known as the "co-hong", they formed an association of about a dozen merchants responsible for most of the foreign trade. They were men of considerable property, who acted as guarantors for the payment of the emperor's customs of entrance as well as all other duties and fees on the import and export cargoes and the various charges enforced during the time the trading vessel lay at Whampoa. Sealing captains arriving before 1800, and without a supercargo, dealt directly with the hong merchants or transacted their business with them through the American consul at Canton or other individuals there with experience in the trade. Captain Metcalf sold the first American shipment of seal skins in 1788 through a private English trader who served as the Prussian consul at Canton; a decade later, Captain Fanning sold the skins he obtained at Más Afuera through another New York ship's master who was at Canton at the same time and had been there twice before. But the following year, in 1799, a twenty-one-year-old Bostonian, Sullivan Dorr, settled at Canton as a private agent. Remaining at the Chinese trading capital through the heyday of sealing at Más Afuera, he negotiated the sale of many cargoes of skins taken in the Southeastern Pacific by vessels whose masters were inexperienced in the trade or did not carry supercargoes.

The sealing captain or his supercargo were also required to engage a "comprador" and an interpreter. The comprador provided the food and provisions for the captain and officers who resided at the factory, or warehouse, at Canton and for the crew and officers that remained on the vessel downriver at Whampoa. The interpreter transacted the ship's business with the customs house, to which no foreigners were admitted, and maintained communication with the other officials, who avoided direct contact with Westerners. The sealing vessel *Favourite* paid its interpreter over five hundred dollars; however, the fee also included the percentage the interpreter received from the sale of any part of a ship's cargo at Canton not consigned directly to the fiador. For while the Yankee captain or his supercargo usually sold the entire cargo of skins or sandalwood through the hong merchant who was acting as his security, it was not a requirement. One New York vessel disposed of most of its cargo through "the

Black Doctor," who traded with the privileges and responsibilities of a fiador or hong merchant although not himself a member of that association. The term "chop" was generally extended to include the duty placed on a trading item while specifically it meant the mark or stamp of the hong merchant required to appear on every article traded at Canton; it was the means by which the interpreter computed the customs for each trading vessel.

As soon as the hong merchant agreed upon a price for the seal skins or sandalwood, the cargo was hoisted from the ship into sampans supplied by the interpreter. The sampans carried the cargo upriver to the outskirts of Canton where it was deposited in the factory, or hong, hired by the captain or his agent. The master and the supercargo followed the sampans in one of the vessel's small boats and spent most of their time in the factory until the return cargo was completed; the crew remained on the vessel at Whampoa, going up to Canton whenever leave was granted. The American and European hongs occupied a stretch along the Pearl River in the suburb; no foreigners were officially allowed in the city itself. Each factory was approached from the river through a flight of steps and a gate and connected with the quay which ran the length of the hong area. The foreign factories contained a number of sub-units—also called "factories"—which included storage space for cargoes, a dining hall and sleeping quarters for the captain and the supercargo as well as accommodations for the comprador and the numerous servants, cooks, and coolies. The rental of the six units in the American factory ranged from twelve hundred to three hundred and fifty dollars for the trading period.

Sometimes the sealing captain shared a factory with a fellow American or, if a factory was not immediately available, he lodged at the "select boarding house" run by a New Englander, Captain William Magee, in a large warehouse rented from the hong merchant Puan-Khequa. Captain Magee was respected among the Chinese for his exploits against the Malayan pirates in the waters off Macao, and his tavern, located close to the factory of the East India Company, was popular with the traders of both English-speaking countries. Captain Magee also owned several sampans which were hired by foreigners to make the two- to three-hour trip between Canton and Whampoa. The sampans were flat bottom boats, narrow at the bow and stern but broad in the beam, carrying a raised, ornamented cabin with a bamboo roof and small shuttered windows. Captain Cook's successor, James King, described the sampans on the Pearl River during his visit to Canton in 1779, remarking on their handsome furnishing, which included chairs, mats, and tables and "a small waxen idol, in a case of gilt leather, before which stood a pot containing lighted tapers made of dry chips, or matches, and gum." [5] He noted the use of joss sticks made from sandalwood two decades before the first Yankee traders reached the mainland of Asia from Vanua Levu.

The price the sealing captain obtained for his skins depended upon a variety of factors, including their quality and condition, the number currently offered or just previously sold, the time of the year, and the strength of competition from the Russians. In the two decades between the arrival of Captain Stewart's cargo of skins from Más Afuera in 1792 and the outbreak of war in 1812, approximately two and one half million seal skins reached the Chinese trading capital from American vessels hunting the oceans of the southern hemisphere. The price of skins fluctuated during this period from a low of forty-two cents per skin received by the unlucky Captain Stewart in 1792 to a high of one dollar and twelve cents per skin obtained in 1801 by Captain Obed Wyer in the *Concord* of Salem.[6] The peak years were between 1800 and 1803, when over a million skins arrived from the seal islands below the equator and were bartered for nine hundred thousand dollars in teas and other merchandise. Captain Wyer's high price of one dollar and twelve cents per skin was obtained shortly before the beginning of the Chinese New Year, when it was customary for the hong merchants to dispose of current goods and settle their accounts. The skins from the *Betsey* of Boston had sold for eighty-five cents each a month before; the skins from the *Hope* of New Haven sold at ninety cents each at the beginning of 1802.

Although the American hunters brought a million seal skins to Canton in the three peak years, the average selling price of ninety cents apiece for this period compares favorably with the average for the two decades between 1792 and 1812. The skins Captain Josiah Roberts obtained in the first Yankee expedition to the islands of San Ambrosio and San Félix brought sixty cents each in 1792; the cargo Captain Edmund Fanning carried to China from Más Afuera in 1798 realized fifty cents per skin. In 1800, Captain William Howell arrived at Canton with a lading of one hundred and ten thousand skins, the result of more than two years' labor on Más Afuera by a gang from New Haven, and he was described as "a little displeased" with the expected price of eighty cents apiece.[7] This cargo, the largest single haul brought to the Chinese trading capital from the hunting grounds of the southern hemisphere, accounted for more than one-tenth of the skins sold by Yankee traders in the peak years between 1800 and 1803. The supply declined sharply in 1804; the cargo hoisted out of the *Lady Adams* of Nantucket that year and shipped upriver from Whampoa in four "chop boats," each carrying about fifteen thousand skins, was one of the last substantial shipments from the Southeastern Pacific. The figure again rose briefly between 1810 and 1812 when some of the Northwest fur traders brought seal skins along with their more valuable cargo of sea-otter skins. Captain John Ebbets recorded an agreement with the hong merchant Kinqua in 1811 for "undressed seal skins" at two dollars apiece; the skins were purchased in barter from the Indians of the Russian settlements in Alaska.[8]

The dozen Yankee vessels that carried sandalwood to Canton from Fiji in the years between 1805 and 1812 sold their cargoes for an average of seventeen dollars a picul, an Oriental weight equivalent to one and one-third pounds. The selling price was stable over this period; relatively few vessels were involved annually in the trade at Fiji and the commodity was always held in high repute by the Chinese. The use of sandalwood in China antedates the importation of the tea shrub by many centuries. The fragrant heartwood of the tree was ground into a fine powder and glued on sticks or paper for use as incense for religious ceremonies and funeral rites. The widespread use of sandalwood, the great scarcity of the sandalwood tree, and the nature of the trade at Fiji made it a highly profitable commodity in the Canton market. The sealing vessel *Criterion*, which carried the initial American shipment from Fiji to Canton in 1805, sold a cargo that cost only fifteen hundred dollars to obtain on Sandalwood Island for about eighty thousand dollars' worth of teas, silks, and porcelain. The last Yankee vessel to reach the Chinese trading capital with sandalwood from Fiji, the *Hunter* of Boston, disposed of a similar cargo for an equivalent value in merchandise although her master obtained his wood in the vicinity of Wailea Bay for less than one thousand dollars.

The price the hong merchant designated for a cargo of sandalwood or seal skins determined the captain's barter in teas and other merchandise at the City of Rams, the ancient name for Canton. Most of the cargo was traded for tea, the item that first brought the Americans to the Far East. The tea shrub had been introduced to China at least a thousand years before the Yankees reached the Orient. Among the many legends concerning the origin of tea, one relates the story of Bodhidharma and the plant as a symbol of attention or wakefulness. Bodhidharma, who came to China from India early in the sixth century to teach the doctrine of Gautama Buddha, vowed to pass sleepless years in prayer and meditation. One day, however, he fell asleep; overcome by a sense of his weakness before the task he had set for himself, Bodhidharma cut off his eyelids and threw them on the ground. The Buddha caused them to grow from the earth as the tea shrub whose leaves seem to resemble eyelids, and when dried and steeped in water the resulting brew hinders sleep. The custom of serving tea at all official and private gatherings originated during the Sung dynasty, when tea became China's social and ceremonial drink. By the time the colonist gained independence from England, tea was among the most significant of America's imports.

A merchant of New York active in the China trade estimates that his countrymen consumed an average of four million pounds of tea annually in the ten years between 1795 and 1805.[9] About half of the tea was black Bohea and two-fifths was green Hyson and Gun Powder, the superior leaves of the Hyson "formed into hard round curls or knots the size of shot." [10] Only a small quantity of the expensive black Souchong was exported to America; most of the tea sold to the Yankee traders under this name was the "Anchoy Souchong" which had the flavor and appearance of the highest quality Souchong but soon lost its fine virtues. The green Hyson and the black Souchong were sold to the trading captains at Canton in a completely cured state and already stored in chests. The popular Bohea arrived at the trading capital partially cured and was then dried in the cool weather of late fall and early winter. After the sealing captain completed his purchases of Bohea, the baskets were delivered to his factory to be packed into chests.

The chests were deposited at the warehouse the evening previous to packing and set along the floor. The captain and his supercargo, or agent or other officer who helped transact the business, were up at dawn to make sure the tea they purchased was packed into the chests assigned to them. A basket of Bohea was emptied into every chest, then a coolie stepped into each packing case and began to tread the tea into powder, "and thus do 200 naked Devils continue till 12 oclock wrighing and twisting to give the greatest force to their feet, during which one is almost suffocated with the powder or dust which is raised from the Tea." [11] The Yankees discovered that the coolies tried to protect their feet with a shoe which damaged the tea by grinding it into too fine a powder. "We generally walk among them," writes the supercargo of the *Neptune* in 1798, "and if they do not readily lift up their feet to show they have nothing on we give them a rap over the shins." [12] The Americans discovered that some of the rented factories had trap doors over the packing area from which old and inferior tea was showered down into the chests amid the dust from the treading. "The Cooleys & Boatmen," warned a Yankee trader at Canton in 1806, "often play Tricks, & you should not be surprised if in a Cargo a chest or two should prove Chaff." [13] The traders also complained of the large number of packing cases the coolies destroyed in the process of grinding the tea into powder.

The principal trading item after tea was cloth fabric, mainly black and colored silk for women's wear and blue, white, and yellow nankeen for men's clothing. The sealing captains also purchased toys (including children's tea sets), chessmen, sugar candy, artificial flowers, window blinds, and umbrellas and fans made from sandalwood, ivory, and tortoise shell. They contracted for large quantities of chinaware, either as general merchandise or under special order. "Madam, agreeable to your request at my departure from America," wrote Sullivan Dorr from Canton in 1799 to Mary Pope in Boston, "have procured one tea and coffee sett of china ware containing 84 pieces also 1 pair pitchers and two mugs. had I agreeable to memo. given, had them cypherd, the money would not have procured the tea and coffee sett, therefore you must excuse the omission." [14] Tea sets of fifty pieces sold at Canton for about three dollars; "table" sets of one hundred and seventy pieces sold for approximately twenty-two dollars, those of the best quality blue and white Nankeen brought ninety dollars; the price was double when the porcelain was ordered with a painted cipher. Despite the additional cost, a great deal of chinaware with the armorial bearings of old England as well as the American eagle and shield was brought home in sealing vessels to New York and New England. The shipmasters also purchased paintings depicting the foreign factories at Canton and views of Whampoa and Boca Tigre; and commissioned paintings on glass which displayed the seals of the different states, emblems of the Masonic Order and the Society of Cincinnatus as well as various patriotic scenes.

While trading at Canton, foreigners and their ships' crews were confined to the quay in front of the factory area, about a quarter of a mile along the river, and to a few surrounding streets entirely occupied by stores. The principal thoroughfare was China Street, paved with small stones and lined with two-story buildings that housed a store on the first floor and workshops, warehouses, and some lodgings on the second floor. The natives of Canton did not live in the suburban area to which foreigners were restricted; they returned at night to the city. Sometimes, American traders were taken by the mandarins a short distance into the city of Canton itself. Captain Fanning recounts going through one of the gates with a high official and being surrounded almost immediately by a mob who showered him with dirt, rags, and bones; he was able to cross into the suburban factory area only after the official's bodyguards held the populace back with bamboo staves. The Yankee mariners who strayed alone into the forbidden city often had a difficult time returning to the restricted area where they were tolerated. Several seamen from the *Betsey* of New Haven escaped back into the suburb from an angry crowd in Canton by tossing coins over their shoulders, reaching the gate, according to their account, just as the money was exhausted.

The money the Yankee seamen used for their personal expenditures at Canton was the Spanish dollar. Cut or broken into pieces, the parts of the dollar served as change, the value determined by the weight of each piece. The merchant always carried scales and weights with him as well as a pair of scissors to cut the silver coin. As soon as a ship's master made the cash advance in Spanish silver dollars to his crew for their own private trading, the men purchased "Chinese dresses and paraded about the suburbs."[15] The sailor from a Boston sealing and trading adventure who made this observation added that his own dress was of "sky-blue silk." The ships' account books kept at Canton revealed fairly large sums paid to tailors; the men stowed the silk garments carefully in their sea-chests when they departed and wore them when the vessel reached the home port. A citizen of New York recalled the arrival of the little brig *Betsey:* "The crew, some twenty odd in number, appeared to be all active young Americans and also all wearing their China silk jackets made a striking impression on the crowds gathered each day she was unloading." [16]

The seamen used a part of their cash advance at Canton to buy items to resell at home or for members of their family and friends. A seal hunter from the *Favourite* of Nantucket listed his purchases in 1807: "2 umbrellas at $5, 3 parasols at $3.75, and 3 pieces silk at $36.50." [17] They spent a certain portion of their advance on what they called "samshew," the whiskey produced locally for visiting seamen. The men also indulged in the luxury of bird's nest soup but admitted the ingredient too subtle for their taste. Among other purchases, the Yankee sailors selected caged birds of brilliant plumage which they carried back to their vessels at Whampoa. A New Haven sealer, who left his cage of birds on deck during a storm, returned to find them dingy creatures from whose feathers all the bright paint had been washed off in the rain. Complaints of "boxes packed with rolls of paper instead of silks" and "chests filled with chips instead of teas" indicate that deception was practiced equally on the trading masters and their seamen.[18]

While the captain and supercargo lived mainly in the factory at Canton, the crew remained on the vessel at Whampoa. Their principal occupation was overhauling the ship for the homeward voyage. During the time the vessel lay downriver from Canton, the men were supplied with provisions by the comprador who also provided the stores and food for the factory. The provisions included beef, pork, chicken, goose, fish, eggs, milk, bread, fruit, salad, condiments, candy, and ginger. The men had a certain leisure at Whampoa; a New England seamen recorded spending part of his time there painting the cabin floor "in marble diamonds." [19] The occupants of the factory at Canton seemed to feel the restrictiveness of their confinement more strongly than the men at Whampoa. They spent their leisure walking on the quay and visiting and dining with each other and with some of the British captains, supercargoes, and residents of the community. Captain Samuel Hill of Boston fell under the influence of one of the Englishmen, a missionary, and was "saved" in Canton in 1811. "I pass over thousands of instances of depravity and folly," confessed the sandalwood trader as he recorded the story of his conversion.[20] At this time Captain Hill discarded his copies of Voltaire and Thomas Paine in favor of religious tracts.

The crews at Whampoa also visited a good deal among themselves. "The mates dined on board *America* had our boat to row them about after dinner." With this reference to one of the vessels owned by the Lords of the Pacific, who were at Whampoa with their cargoes of sandalwood from Hawaii and seal skins from California, a New England seaman continued in his journal: "Went on board ship *America* to dinner then went on board the English transport *Indefatigable* ashore on board *America* took supper." [21] The mariners also hired their own boats from the comprador; the boatswain on a New Haven sealing vessel spent fifty dollars in one afternoon of 1799 for a sampan to carry him from ship to ship where he treated his fellow Yankees to liberal portions of the raw whiskey of Canton. A more sobering side of the little community of American vessels at Whampoa was the death of a sailor. "Attended a funeral from the Ship Stranger," noted a Nantucket seaman.[22] Both the latter vessel and his own *Lady Adams* had reached China in 1804 from the seal islands of the Southeastern Pacific.

The sealing vessels lay at Whampoa from one to three months, depending on the length of time necessary to complete the return cargo for America. When all the business was finished, the captain obtained the "Chow Chow Chop," the final clearance for goods, stores, and baggage that still remained at the factory in the suburbs. This was the last chance to bring any articles downriver from Canton, and the ship's master usually distributed a good supply of wine among the mandarins to prevent any trouble in his closing encounter with the officials of the Heavenly Dynasty. As the firing of salutes had been forbidden at Whampoa after several fatal accidents, the sealers waved and shouted as the vessel slipped from the anchorage and dropped down toward the first bar. Several days later, she cleared the "Tiger's Gate" and ran into the South China Sea. The passage was dangerous as far as the Sunda Strait, which was more or less the limit of the pirates' hunting ground. With Java Head safely behind, the sealing vessel struck out across the Indian Ocean for the North American homeland.

Bibliographical Notes

1. The Goal

1. Henry Knox *Papers,* Massachusetts Historical Society. Letter to Henry Knox from John Coffin Jones, August 7, 1791.
2. Amasa Delano, *A Narrative of Voyages and Travels, in the Northern and Southern Hemispheres*, Boston, 1817, p. 542.
3. John A. Ledyard, *A Journal of Captain Cook's Last Voyage to the Pacific Ocean,* Hartford, 1783, p. 70.
4. Jared Sparks, *The Life of John Ledyard,* Cambridge, 1828, p. 131.
5. Journal of the *Empress of China*, Historical Society of Pennsylvania.
6. Constable-Pierrepont *Papers,* New York Public Library. Account Book of the *Mary*.
7. Peter Osbeck, *A Voyage to China and the East Indies,* 2 vols., London, 1771, I, p. 233.
8. John White Smith, "Letter to his father dated Canton, December 3, 1784," *Pennsylvania Magazine of History and Biography,* Vol. 9 (1885), p. 485.
9. Papers of the *Experiment,* New-York Historical Society.
10. John Meares, *Voyages Made in the Year 1788 and 1789*, London, 1790, p. lxxxvi.
11. C. P. Claret Fleurieu, *A Voyage Round the World Performed During the Year 1790, 1791 and 1792 by Étienne Marchand,* 2 vols., London, 1801, I, p. cxlvii.

12. Sullivan Dorr, *Memorandum Book, Canton, 1801,* Rhode Island Historical Society.
13. "The Diary of Ebenezer Townsend, Jr.," New Haven Colony Historical Society *Papers,* Vol. IV, 1888, p. 28.
14. Nathaniel Portlock, *A Voyage Round the World,* London, 1789, p. 37.
15. "Diary of Ebenezer Townsend, Jr.," p. 28.
16. *The Journals of Major Samuel Shaw, with a Life of the Author by Josiah Quincy,* Boston, 1847, p. 296.
17. Samuel Blodget, *Economica: A Statistical Manual for the United States of America,* Washington, 1806, p. 70.

2. The Hunted

1. Dorr Family *Papers,* Massachusetts Historical Society. Instructions to Captain Edes, September 11, 1799.
2. Journal of the *Jefferson,* Massachusetts Historical Society.
3. George Anson, *A Voyage Round the World,* London, 1748, p. 122.
4. John Hawkesworth, *An Account of the Voyages for making Discoveries in the Southern Hemisphere,* 3 vols., London, 1773, I, p. 556.
5. Ibid. I, p. 14.
6. Samuel Hill, *Autobiographical Notes,* New York Public Library.
7. Sir George Staunton, *An Authentic Account of an Embassy to the Emperor of China,* 2 vols., Philadelphia, 1799, I, p. 104.
8. Thomas Falkner, *A Description of Patagonia,* Hereford, 1774, p. 73.
9. *Historical Records of New Zealand,* Vol. I, II, Wellington, 1908, 1914, I, p. 273 (quotes Sir Joseph Banks).
10. Antoine Joseph Pernety, *The History of a Voyage to the Malouine (or Falkland) Islands,* London, 1773, p. 203.
11. [P. F.] Péron, *Mémoires du Captaine Péron, sur ses voyages,* 2 vols., Paris, 1824, I, p. 188.
12. "When excited, their motions are very quick—like the flash of a gun on touching the match: hence the name of *clap-match.*" Benjamin Morrell, *A Narrative of Four Voyages,* New York, 1832, p. 76.
13. James Cook, *A Voyage towards the South Pole, and Round the World,* 2 vols., London, 1777, II, p. 203.
14. Edmund Fanning, *Voyages Round the World,* New York, 1833, p. 26.
15. David Forbes, *Journal 1797–1800,* New Haven Colony Historical Society.
16. Pernety, *The History of a Voyage . . . ,* p. 201.
17. George Little, *Life on the Ocean; or, Twenty Years at Sea,* Boston, 1845, p. 107.

18. Staunton, *An Authentic Account of an Embassy . . .*, I, p. 105.
19. Fleurieu, *A Voyage Round the World . . .*, I, p. cxlvii.
20. "Nathaniel Appleton's Journal of the Voyage of the Ship Concord Around the World," Essex Institute, *Historical Collections*, Vol. 83, 1947, p. 161.
21. *Historical Records of New South Wales*, Vol. I–VII, Sydney, 1893–1901, V, p. 423.
22. J. H. Tuckey, *An Account of a Voyage*, London, 1805, p. 122.

3. The Hunters

1. Amasa Delano, *A Narrative of Voyages and Travels . . .*, p. 320.
2. "Nathaniel Appleton's Journal . . . ," p. 161.
3. Gouverneur and Kemble, *Letter-Book 1796–1798*, New York Public Library. Letter to William Rotch & Sons, New York, July 1, 1797.
4. Journal of the *Asia*, Marine Historical Association, Mystic, Conn.
5. Charles H. Barnard, *A Narrative of the Sufferings and Adventures of Capt. Charles H. Barnard*, New York, 1829, p. 2.
6. "Diary of Ebenezer Townsend, Jr.," p. 101.
7. Alexander Starbuck, *The History of Nantucket*, Boston, 1924, p. 410.
8. Lucy Brewer, *The Female Marine*, 1816, p. 39.
9. Almira Paul, *The Surprising Adventures of Almira Paul*, New York, 1840, p. 15.
10. "Diary of Ebenezer Townsend, Jr.," p. 102.
11. Account Book of the *Betsey*, American Geographical Society, New York City.
12. Delano, *A Narrative of Voyages and Travels . . .*, p. 421.
13. Joel Root, *Journal*, New-York Historical Society.
14. Physicians Agreement on Ship *Sally*, New Haven Colony Historical Society.
15. Forbes, *Journal*.
16. A. Howard Clark, "The Antarctic Fur-Seal and Sea-Elephant Industries," *The Fisheries and Fishery Industries of the United States*, George Brown Goode, editor, Section V, Volume II, Washington, 1887, p. 444.
17. Journal of the *Eliza*, Peabody Museum, Salem.
18. Journal of the *Betsey*, New Haven Colony Historical Society.
19. Account Book of the *Dromo*, Baker Library, Harvard University.
20. Journal of the *New Hazard*, Peabody Museum, Salem.
21. "Nathaniel Appleton's Journal . . . ," p. 157.

4. The South Atlantic

1. Barnard, *A Narrative of the Sufferings . . .* , p. 261.
2. Falkner, *A Description of Patagonia,* p. 95.
3. "Nathaniel Appleton's Journal . . . ," p. 155.
4. Pernety, *The History of a Voyage . . .* , p. 201.
5. George Foster, *A Voyage Round the World,* 2 vols., London, 1777, II, p. 530.
6. Fanning *Papers,* American Geographical Society, New York City. Memorial to the 26th Congress of the United States.
7. Elijah Davis, *Journal at the Falklands,* New Haven Colony Historical Society.
8. Ibid.
9. Foster, *A Voyage Round the World,* II, p. 529.
10. Forbes, *Journal.*
11. Journal of the *Diana,* Essex Institute, Salem, Mass.
12. Clark, "The Antarctic Fur-Seal . . . ," p. 444.
13. "Diary of Ebenezer Townsend, Jr.," p. 34.
14. Ibid. p. 34.
15. Bernard Penrose, *An Account of the Last Expedition to Port Egmont,* London, 1775, p. 31.
16. Pernety, *The History of a Voyage . . .* , p. 246.
17. Edmund Fanning, *Voyages to the South Seas, Indian and Pacific Oceans,* New York, 1838, p. 82.
18. "Diary of Ebenezer Townsend, Jr.," p. 20.
19. Forbes, *Journal.*
20. Mrs. Theodore Roosevelt, Kermit Roosevelt, *American Backlogs,* New York, 1928, p. 65.
21. William Moulton, *A Concise Extract, from the Sea Journal of William Moulton,* Utica, 1804, p. 27.
22. "Diary of Ebenezer Townsend, Jr.," p. 38.
23. Ibid. p. 40.

5. The Indian Ocean

1. *The Oriental Navigator,* Philadelphia, 1801, p. 60.
2. George Mortimer, *Observations and Remarks Made During a Voyage,* London, 1791, p. 14.

3. J. J. H. Labillardiere, *Voyage in Search of La Pérouse*, 2 vols., London, 1800, I, p. 155.
4. Journal of the *Warren*, Marine Historical Association, Mystic, Conn.
5. Samuel Holmes, *The Journal of Mr. Samuel Holmes*, London, 1798, p. 29.
6. Staunton, *An Authentic Account* . . . , I, p. 113.
7. John Barrow, *A Voyage to Cochinchina*, London, 1806, p. 156.
8. Péron, *Mémoires du Captaine* . . . , I, p. 217.
9. Ibid. I, p. 284.
10. "Letters of Sullivan Dorr," Massachusetts Historical Society *Proceedings*, Vol. 67, 1941–44, p. 227.
11. Péron, *Memoires du Capitaine*. . . , I, p. 305.
12. James Cook (and James King), *A Voyage to the Pacific Ocean*, 3 vols., London, 1785, I, p. 83.
13. John Bartlett *Journal*, Peabody Museum, Salem.
14. Journal of the *Asia*.
15. Fanning, *Voyages Round the World*, p. 315.
16. Charles Medyett Goodridge, *Narrative of a Voyage to the South Seas*, London, 1832, p. 40.

6. Más Afuera

1. "Nathaniel Appleton's Journal . . . ," p. 230.
2. Root, *Journal*.
3. "Robert Haswell's Log of the First Voyage of the *Columbia*," Massachusetts Historical Society *Collections*, Vol. 79 (1941), p. 24.
4. "Diary of Ebenezer Townsend, Jr.," p. 48.
5. Forbes, *Journal*.
6. Fanning, *Voyages Round the World*, p. 109.
7. Forbes, *Journal*.
8. Journal of the *Lady Adams*, Mr. Albert G. Brock, Nantucket.
9. "Nathaniel Appleton's Journal . . . ," p. 228.
10. Elijah Davis, *Journal on Massafuera*, New Haven Colony Historical Society.
11. Forbes, *Journal*.
12. Davis, *Journal*.
13. Forbes, *Journal*.
14. Delano, *A Narrative of Voyages and Travels* . . . , p. 306.
15. Forbes, *Journal*.

16. Davis, *Journal.*
17. Journal of the *Minerva,* Marine Historical Association, Mystic, Conn.
18. Davis, *Journal.*
19. Forbes, *Journal.*
20. Davis, *Journal.*
21. "Diary of Ebenezer Townsend, Jr.," p. 49.
22. Moulton, *A Concise Extract . . .* , p. 107.
23. "Diary of Ebenezer Townsend, Jr.," p. 48.
24. Forbes, *Journal.*
25. Journal of the *Minerva.*
26. Journal of the *Rebecca,* Marine Historical Association, Mystic, Conn.
27. Forbes, *Journal.*
28. "Diary of Ebenezer Townsend, Jr.," p. 49.
29. Forbes, *Journal.*
30. Davis, *Journal.*
31. Forbes, *Journal.*
32. Ibid.
33. Davis, *Journal.*
34. Barnard, *A Narrative of the Sufferings . . .* , p. 201.
35. Moulton, *A Concise Extract . . .* , p. 66.
36. Journal of the *Minerva.*
37. Forbes, *Journal.*
38. Root, *Journal.*

7. The Southeastern Pacific

1. Journal of the *Jefferson.*
2. James Colnett, *A Voyage to the South Atlantic and Round the Horn,* London, 1798, p. 33.
3. Journal of the *Minerva.*
4. "Nathaniel Appleton's Journal . . . , p. 161.
5. Captain Asa Dodge of the *Alexander,* Sullivan Dorr *Letters,* p. 246.
6. Journal of the *Jefferson.*
7. Richard J. Cleveland, *A Narrative of Voyages and Commercial Enterprises,* Boston, 1850, p. 174.
8. Delano, *A Narrative of Voyages and Travels . . .* , p. 507.
9. Moulton, *A Concise Extract . . .* , p. 104.
10. Journal of the *Minerva.*

11. "Nathaniel Appleton's Journal . . . ," p. 235.
12. The *Miantonomah,* Norwich, Captain Valentine Swain.
13. The *Onico,* Norwich, Captain George Howe.
14. Moulton, *A Concise Extract* . . . , p. 101.
15. "Nathaniel Appleton's Journal . . . ," pp. 158, 159.
16. Delano, *A Narrative of Voyages and Travels* . . . , p. 283.
17. John Myers, *The Life, Voyages and Travels of John Myers,* London, 1817, p. 138.
18. The *Rebecca,* New York, Captain Uriel Coffin.
19. The *Huron,* New Haven, Captain William Moulthrop.
20. Delano, *A Narrative of Voyages and Travels* . . . , p. 299.
21. Journal of the *Dispatch,* Connecticut Historical Society, Hartford.
22. David Porter (Captain), *Journal of a Cruise Made to the Pacific Ocean,* 2 vols., New York, 1822, I, p. 129.
23. Little, *Life on the Ocean* . . . , p. 71.
24. Isaac Iselin, *Journal of a Trading Voyage Around the World,* New York, p. 12.
25. Journal of the Voyage of *H.M.S. Tagus,* New York Public Library.
26. Porter, *Journal of a Cruise* . . . , I, p. 136.
27. Little, *Life on the Ocean* . . . , p. 93.
28. Reference is to Philip Carteret, Hawkesworth's *Voyages.*
29. Journal of the *Topaz,* Nantucket Whaling Museum.

8. Australasia

1. Benjamin Carter, *Journal,* Rhode Island Historical Society.
2. Papers of the *Favourite,* Nantucket Whaling Museum.
3. David Collins, *An Account of the English Colony in New South Wales,* 2 vols., London, 1798, 1802, I, p. 254.
4. *Historical Records of New South Wales,* II, p. 2n (cited hereafter as H.R.N.S.W.).
5. Collins, *An Account of the English Colony* . . . , I, p. 260.
6. H.R.N.S.W., IV, p. 83.
7. *Historical Records of Australia,* Series I, Vols. I–VIII, Sydney, 1914–1916, V, p. 671 (cited hereafter as H.R.A.).
8. Delano, *A Narrative of Voyages and Travels* . . . , p. 320.
9. H.R.N.S.W., III, p. 30.
10. Ibid. IV, p. 871.
11. John Turnbull, *A Voyage Round the World,* London, 1813, p. 70.

12. Journal of the *Fanny,* Peabody Museum, Salem.
13. H.R.N.S.W., IV, p. 890.
14. H.R.A., IV, p. 145.
15. Delano, *A Narrative of Voyages and Travels* . . . , p. 421.
16. Fanning, *Voyages Round the World,* p. 318.
17. The *Argo* was owned by Robert Berry, an English merchant at Macao.
18. Basil Thomson, *South Sea Yarns,* Edinburgh and London, 1894, p. 291.
19. Joseph Waterhouse, *The King and People of Fiji,* London, 1866, p. 22.
20. Thomson, *South Sea Yarns,* p. 292.
21. H.R.A., V, p. 16.
22. H.R.N.S.W., V, p. 514.
23. "The Journal of William Lockerby," Hakluyt Society *Works,* Sec. Ser., No. LII, London, 1925, p. 188.
24. H.R.A., V, p. 697.

9. Fiji

1. William Bligh, *Voyage to the South Sea,* London, 1792, p. 182.
2. *Salem Register,* August 4, 1800, Vol. I, No. 25.
3. William Mariner, *An Account of the Natives of the Tonga Islands,* 2 vols., London, 1817, I, p. 303.
4. Cook, *A Voyage towards the South Pole* . . . , II, p. 19.
5. Lockerby's Journal, p. lxxxviii.
6. Admiralty Court Records of Vessels Captured by British Men-of-War and Privateers 1778–1808, Peabody Museum, Salem. Briefs of the *Jenny.*
7. [William Wilson], *A Missionary Voyage in the Ship Duff,* London, 1799, p. 289.
8. Log of the *Hope,* Baker Library, Harvard University.
9. Lockerby's Journal, p. lxxxviii.
10. Fanning, *Voyages to the South Seas* . . . , p. 123.
11. Ibid. p. 62.
12. Samuel Patterson, *Narrative of the Adventures and Sufferings of Samuel Patterson,* Palmer, 1817, p. 83.
13. "Journal of the Missionaries," Hakluyt Society *Works,* Sec. Ser., No. LII, London, 1925, p. 144.
14. Lockerby's Journal, p. 22.
15. Ibid. p. 42.

16. Fanning, *Voyages to the South Seas . . .*, p. 59.
17. Patterson, *Narrative of the Adventures . . .*, p. 85.
18. Ibid. p. 97.
19. "Tatawaqa—Charlie Savage," Fijian Society *Transactions*, Suva, 1912–1913, p. 1.
20. Ibid. p. 3.
21. Patterson, *Narrative of the Adventures . . .*, p. 101.
22. Mariner, *An Account of the Natives . . .*, II, p. 72.
23. H.R.N.S.W., V, p. 620.
24. The *Fair American,* while sailing under American colors, was registered in Manila and owned by an Englishman.
25. Peter Dillion, *Narrative and Successful Result of a Voyage in the South Seas,* 2 vols., London, 1829, I, p. 2.

10. Polynesia

1. Porter, *Journal of a Cruise . . .*, II, p. 22.
2. Log of the *Jefferson* (Belknap 179?), Massachusetts Historical Society.
3. Joseph Ingraham, "An Account of a recent discovery of Seven Islands in the South Pacific Ocean," Massachusetts Historical Society *Collections,* Vol. II, 1793, p. 21.
4. Fanning, *Voyages Round the World,* p. 185.
5. "Diary of Ebenezer Townsend, Jr.," p. 53.
6. Cook (and James King), *A Voyage to the Pacific Ocean,* III, p. 46.
7. "The Hope's Track Among the Sandwich Islands," Hawaiian Historical Society *Reprints,* No. 3, 1918, p. 25.
8. Barnard, *A Narrative of the Sufferings . . .*, p. 219.
9. Iselin, *Journal of a Trading Voyage . . .*, p. 79.
10. John Nicol, *The Life and Adventures of John Nicol, Mariner,* Edinburgh, 1822, p. 71.
11. Journal of the *New Hazard.*
12. Journal of the *Betsey,* New Haven Colony Historical Society.
13. Little, *Life on the Ocean . . .*, p. 131.
14. "Diary of Ebenezer Townsend, Jr.," p. 59.
15. Iselin, *Journal of a Trading Voyage . . .*, p. 78.
16. Journal at Waimea, Massachusetts Historical Society.
17. Solid Men of Boston in the Northwest, Bancroft Library, University of California, Berkeley.
18. Edwin Welles Dwight, *Memoirs of Henry Obookiah,* New Haven, 1818.

19. John J. Astor *Papers,* Baker Library, Harvard University. Vol. XX, Captain William Pigot to John Ebbets, January 7, 1816.
20. "The Hope's Track . . . ," p. 16.
21. J. & T. H. Perkins, *Letter Book 1807–1815,* Massachusetts Historical Society. Letter to Perkins & Co., Canton, May 18, 1807.
22. *The North American Review,* Vol. III, Boston, 1816, p. 53.
23. Journal at Waimea.
24. Journal of the *Betsey.*
25. Fanning, *Voyages Round the World,* p. 237.
26. "Diary of Ebenezer Townsend, Jr.," p. 80.

11. Canton

1. Journal of the *Empress of China.*
2. *The Journals of Major Samuel Shaw* . . . , p. 242.
3. Little, *Life on the Ocean* . . . , p. 148.
4. Papers of the *Favourite.*
5. Cook (and James King), *A Voyage to the Pacific Ocean,* III, p. 426.
6. The supercargo of the *Neptune* claimed he sold the cargo of eighty thousand skins at Canton for three dollars each. The *Betsey* of New York, leaving Más Afuera a month ahead of the *Neptune,* discharged a cargo of "prime seal skins" at Canton which sold on September 22, 1798, at fifty cents apiece. (Account Book of the *Betsey,* American Geographical Society). The *Neptune* was at Canton in October, November, and December of the same year.
7. Journal of the *Betsey.*
8. Astor *Papers,* Vol. XXXIII. Agreement Between Captain John Ebbets and Kingqua, January 13, 1811.
9. Oliver Wolcott, *Letter-Book 1803–1808,* New York Public Library.
10. Constable-Pierrepont *Papers.* "Notes on the Trade of China, 1796."
11. Ibid.
12. "Diary of Ebenezer Townsend, Jr.," p. 94.
13. Robert Waln *Collection,* Library Company of Philadelphia. John Gibson's "Observations on the Trade with China, 1807."
14. "Letters of Sullivan Dorr," Vol. 67, p. 203.
15. Little, *Life on the Ocean* . . . , p. 149.
16. *Betsey's Voyage from New York Around the World,* New York, 1833, p. 7.

17. Papers of the *Favourite.*
18. Simon Gratz *Papers,* Historical Society of Pennsylvania. Edward Gray to Chonqua, 1809; Willing & Francis vs. Consequa.
19. Journal of the *New Hazard.*
20. Hill, *Autobiographical Notes.*
21. Journal of the *New Hazard.*
22. Journal of the *Lady Adams.*

Index